WRITING KEY

English Grammar and Usage for Better Writing

Yasuyuki Kitao / Anthony Allan

KINSEIDO

Kinseido Publishing Co., Ltd.
3-21 Kanda Jimbo-cho, Chiyoda-ku,
Tokyo 101-0051, Japan

Copyright © 2019 by Yasuyuki Kitao
　　　　　　　　　Anthony Allan

All rights reserved. No part of this publication may be reproduced, stored in a retrieval system, or transmitted, in any form or by any means, electronic, mechanical, photocopying, recording or otherwise, without the prior permission of the publisher.

First published 2019 by Kinseido Publishing Co., Ltd.

Cover design	parastyle inc.
Text design & Editorial support	C-leps Co., Ltd.
Illustrations	Kaori Wada

Photo Credit
- Page 10　Avalon/Jiji
- Page 14　AFP/Jiji
- Page 30　AFP/Jiji
- Page 42　EPA/Jiji
- Page 54　© Fabio Formaggio | Dreamstime.com (top)

🎧 音声ファイル無料ダウンロード

http://www.kinsei-do.co.jp/download/4086

この教科書で 🎧 DL 00 の表示がある箇所の音声は、上記 URL または QR コードにて無料でダウンロードできます。自習用音声としてご活用ください。

▶ PC からのダウンロードをお勧めします。スマートフォンなどでダウンロードされる場合は、ダウンロード前に「解凍アプリ」をインストールしてください。
▶ URL は、検索ボックスではなくアドレスバー（URL 表示欄）に入力してください。
▶ お使いのネットワーク環境によっては、ダウンロードできない場合があります。

◎ CD 00　左記の表示がある箇所の音声は、教室用 CD（Class Audio CD）に収録されています。

はしがき

　本書 *Writing Key: English Grammar and Usage for Better Writing* は、英文読解と、文法を軸とした英文作成を通して、英語のライティング力を高めることを目指したテキストです。各ユニットで1つの文法事項を取り上げ、その文法事項を様々なタスクを通して習得できるよう工夫しています。

　すべてのユニットを、以下の6つのセクションで構成しています。

● *Model Essay*
各ユニットでターゲットとする文法項目がちりばめられた200語程度の文章が収められています。活きた文章の中で、ターゲットの文法項目を含んだ文はどのような使い方をするのか、確認してほしいと思います。

● *Grammar for Writing!*
各ユニットでターゲットにしている文法項目を、例文とともに詳しく説明しています。例として本文から取り上げた文だけではなく、他の分かりやすい文も挙げることにより、理解しやすい解説にするように努めました。

● Step 1　Grammar Practice
文の空所に適切な語句を入れるタスクを通して、英語の感覚を理解してもらうことに主眼を置いています。このことから日本語訳を提示せずに、英文の文脈から適切な語句を書き入れる形にしています（Unit 5 と Unit 15 は、当該文法項目との兼ね合いから、少し異なった形式のタスクになっています）。

● Step 2　Create Sentences
語句の並べ替えを通して、当該ユニットの文法項目を理解できるように工夫しています。文の組み立て方を学んでほしいと思います。

● Step 3　Try Writing
日本語の意味に合致する英文を書くタスクです。そのとき「文法的に正しい」という観点だけではなく、より「英語らしい」文になることを意識してもらうために、いくつか語句を提示し、その語句を使って英文を作成する形式にしました。

● **Step 4** *Write about Yourself*
Model Essayから取り出した文の表現を使って、その他に示した2つの例も参考にしながら、自分のことについて自由に英文を書いてもらうタスクです。将来の本格的な英文エッセイにつなげる前段階のタスクとして位置づけています。

　本書の日本語タイトル『英語の感覚をつかむ 文法からライティングへ』にあるように、本書は様々なタスクを通して、英語母語話者が持っている自然な英語の感覚をつかむことができるように努めました。本テキストを活用し、少しでも英語の感覚を認識でき、かつ英文を書くことが楽しくなれば、著者としてはこの上ない喜びです。

　本書を刊行するに当たっては、企画段階では特に金星堂編集部の松本明子様と金星堂営業部の平田英司様にお世話になり、編集および発行段階では、金星堂編集部の蔦原美智様にお世話になりました。蔦原様のきめ細やかなご配慮と的確なコメントが、本テキストをより良いものにしてくださったことは間違いありません。また他の金星堂編集部の皆様にも、各段階でたいへんお世話になりました。ここに感謝申し上げます。

2018年10月
著者

Table of Contents

- **Unit 1　Orange Clothing**　【動詞の用法】 …………………… 6
  シチリア産オレンジの意外な活用法
- **Unit 2　A Reasonable Dream…**　【文の主語】 ……………… 10
  パラリンピックの誕生
- **Unit 3　Japan's Popular Wave**　【時制】 ……………………… 14
  世界の北斎、街角に現る
- **Unit 4　Color Matters**　【形容詞・副詞】 ……………………… 18
  「いいね！」の親指が表すもの
- **Unit 5　Business, Not Bullets**　【名詞】 ……………………… 22
  アフガン駐留米兵のある思いつき
- **Unit 6　Spices for Life!**　【冠詞・数量詞】 …………………… 26
  カレーを食べて、人生にスパイスを！
- **Unit 7　Plastic Planet**　【分詞】 ……………………………… 30
  バリ島の姉妹が地球を救う
- **Unit 8　London Coffee and Lazy Men**　【関係詞】 ………… 34
  "コーヒー中毒"は怠け者を生む?!
- **Unit 9　Jacques' Lung**　【比較】 ……………………………… 38
  海洋探検家ジャック・クストーの夢
- **Unit 10　Disease vs. Hunger**　【助動詞】 …………………… 42
  マラリアとの闘いは終わらない
- **Unit 11　May We Have a Catalog, Please?**　【仮定法】 …… 46
  あなたの赤ちゃん選んでみませんか
- **Unit 12　Bright Little Lights**　【接続詞】 …………………… 50
  メキシコの小さな村を照らす神秘
- **Unit 13　Popular but Penniless**　【不定詞と動名詞】 ……… 54
  名声を得ども…
- **Unit 14　Taxing the Robots**　【受動態】 …………………… 58
  ロボットに課税せよ
- **Unit 15　Sayonara, My Dear**　【強調・倒置・形式主語】 …… 62
  日本初の外国人英語教師

Unit 1: Orange Clothing

➡ 動詞の用法

Model Essay 太字の表現に注意して読みましょう。 🎧 DL 02 💿 CD 02

In recent years, garment makers **have been creating** new products **using** new kinds of textiles. Examples **include** non-iron shirts and lighter and softer clothing that **keeps** us warmer in winter and cooler in summer. Naturally, such advances **are facilitated** by extensive budgets for research and development.

But with far less money, one design student in Sicily, an island in Italy, **developed** an interesting and environmentally friendly textile for **producing** clothes. The island **is** famous for its delicious mandarin oranges and **produces** a large amount annually. Apart from **selling** them, many of the oranges **are squeezed** to **make** juice, which **results** in thousands of tons of waste peel, or skin. Can you **imagine** such mountains of waste from oranges?

For her university graduation project, the student **wanted** to **find** a way to **put** the waste to good use. Then, after **spending** many hours in the university laboratory, she **succeeded** in **using** the peel to **make** silk-like material. Subsequently, she **established** a company in 2014 to **produce** and **sell** the material to makers of garments such as shirts and dresses. Fortunately, her company **is based** in a local juice-making factory, so it **gets** its necessary waste material for free.

Thanks to the student's efforts, Sicily's unwanted *mountains* should **become** smaller and smaller.

Sicily mandarin oranges

Notes

garment 衣類   textile 織物、布地   facilitate 容易にする   budget 予算   Sicily シチリア (イタリア南方の島)   environmentally friendly 環境にやさしい   apart from ～に加えて   squeeze 絞る、圧搾する   result in ～という結果になる   waste 廃物、くず   peel, skin (果物などの) 皮   imagine 想像する、心に描く   laboratory 実験室、研究所   succeed 成功する   subsequently その後、続いて   material 素材、物質   effort 努力、奮闘   unwanted 役に立たない、不必要な

Grammar for Writing!   動詞の用法

❶ 自動詞と他動詞   DL 03   CD03

英語の動詞には、目的語を必要としない「自動詞」と、必要とする「他動詞」があります。

1. Justin **runs** every morning.   ジャスティンは毎朝走っている。
2. Let's see how their idea **develops**.   彼らのアイデアがどのように発展するか見ていこう。
3. One student **developed** a new kind of textile.   ある学生が新しい種類の布地を開発した。
4. She **wanted** to find a way to put the waste to good use.
   彼女は廃物を役に立たせるための方法を見つけたいと思った。
5. I don't **think** my boss will accept my plan.   上司は私の計画を受け入れないと思う。

▶ 自動詞：目的語を必要としません。ただし修飾語句が後に続く場合（① 波線部）と、修飾語句がない場合（②）があります。
▶ 他動詞：動詞の後に必ず名詞句あるいは名詞節が来て（③④⑤下線部）、動詞の目的語になります。

❷ 動詞にとって不可欠な要素   DL 04   CD04

動詞は自動詞・他動詞の区別だけでは十分ではありません。自動詞であっても後に他の要素を必要とするものや、他動詞であっても目的語以外の要素を必要とするものがあります。

6. Making juice from oranges **results** in thousands of tons of waste peel, or skin.
   オレンジからジュースを作ることは何千トンもの皮の廃物をもたらす。
7. Let's **talk** about the matter later.   その問題は後で話しましょう。

▶ result は自動詞ですが、後に前置詞 in から始まる句（下線部）を必要とします。
▶ talk は自動詞で、Let's talk. のように動詞だけで使われるほか、前置詞 about を使って話す内容を述べたり、talk with her のように話し相手を示したりすることが多いです。

8. Sicily's unwanted *mountains* should **become** smaller and smaller.
   シチリアのゴミの山はどんどん小さくなるはずだ。
9. It **sounded** real, but it was not.   それは本当のように聞こえたが、そうではなかった。
10. My teacher **put** some books on the desk.   先生は机の上に本を置いた。
11. Sweaters **keep** us warm in winter.   セーターは冬に私たちを暖かく保ってくれる。

▶ become や sound は自動詞ですが、必ず後に補語（名詞、形容詞など）を必要とします。
▶ put は他動詞ですが、目的語の他に場所を表す句（前置詞句・副詞句）を必要とします。
▶ keep ~ ...「~を…に保つ」の用法では、目的語の後に補語が必要です。

Unit 1   Orange Clothing

Step 1 *Grammar Practice*

以下の英文の（　）には動詞が入ります。文中の要素を手掛かりにして、適切な動詞を選択肢から選び、必要があれば形を変えて記入しましょう。

1. I forgot to (　　　　　) the strawberry cake in the fridge, so it must have gone bad.
2. His proposal (　　　　　) quite good. We should go with it.
3. I make it a rule to (　　　　　) before going to work every morning.
4. The boss says he will (　　　　　) his future plans with us in a couple of days.
5. It was really nice (　　　　　) with you today. Let's keep in touch.

> look　discuss　talk　put　run

 Step 2 *Create Sentences*

日本語の意味に合わせて、（　）内の語句を並べ替えましょう。

1. 早く仕事を片付けて、遊びましょう。
   (finish / quickly / let's / ourselves / enjoy / and / the work).

2. この書類をどこへしまえばよいか分かりません。
   (put / don't / I / should / know / I / documents / these / where).

3. 話している途中で話をさえぎらないでください。
   (talking / don't / am / I / please / me / interrupt / while).

4. 彼は一流のコンピュータソフトウェア会社に就職しました。
   (computer software / he / at / leading / a / his / company / started / career).

5. 僕はそれは素晴らしい案だと思うよ。
   (idea / me / it / a / wonderful / sounds / like / to).

Step 3 Try Writing

日本語の意味に合わせて、[　　]内の語句を使って英文にしましょう。

1. キュリー夫人は科学の面で貢献したことで有名です。[Marie Curie, contributions]
   _____

2. 値段には消費税が含まれています。[include, consumption tax]
   _____

3. 今晩私の家に来ませんか。[want, come over]
   _____

4. 私は今日中に課題を終えるよう頑張っているところです。[get, my work]
   _____

5. このせいで、私は難しい状況になりました。[put, situation]
   _____

Step 4 Write about Yourself

本文の13行目 "she succeeded in using the peel to make silk-like material" のように、あなたが成功したことについて、本文と以下の例を参考に、英語で短い文章を書いてみましょう。

> 例1 I succeeded in passing my driving test yesterday, so I'm planning to go for a drive this weekend.
>
> 例2 I succeeded in writing a new song after a month of hard work. I hope the fans like it.

Unit 2 A Reasonable Dream...

▶ 文の主語

Model Essay 太字の表現に注意して読みましょう。   DL 05   CD 05

In general, people know that the first Olympic Games were held in Ancient Greece. But do we know when **the Paralympic Games** began? Most of us would probably guess **it** was within the last few decades. Their origins, however, can be traced further back in time to one particular spot, sport and doctor.

On July 29th, 1948, **the Stoke Mandeville Hospital in England** held an archery competition for 16 patients in wheelchairs. The patients were veterans of World War II, and **the idea for the event** came from Sir Ludwig Guttmann, a doctor at the hospital. He strongly believed that sport could assist the rehabilitation of his patients and help them develop physical strength. Surprisingly, he was German, but had fled Nazi Germany.

Year by year, **the hospital's competition** gained attention and was even covered by *TIME* magazine in 1953. That year, 3,000 spectators watched 2,000 athletes from eight countries compete in various events. **The competition's continued growth** prompted the first official Paralympic Games, which took place in 1960 in Rome. While **this** marked a great step forward for humanity, wouldn't **it** be nice if all people were born healthy and all illnesses could be cured? Then **there** would be no need for the Paralympic Games at all. Surely **this** is a reasonable dream for everyone.

Neurological surgeon Sir Ludwig Guttmann, founder of the Paralympic Games

Notes

decade 10年間   origin 起源   trace さかのぼって探る、たどる   further さらに   archery 弓術
competition 競技会、競争   patient 患者   veteran 退役軍人、兵役経験者   Sir Ludwig Guttmann ルートヴィヒ・グットマン卿（ドイツ出身のユダヤ系神経学者）   physical strength 体力   spectator 観客   growth 発展、成長   prompt 促す、きっかけを与える   mark a great step forward 大いに前進する   cure 治療する
reasonable 筋の通った、納得できる   [写真下] neurological surgeon 脳神経外科医

Grammar for Writing! 文の主語

❶ 「物・事」が主語に来る例 🎧 DL 06 💿 CD06

日本語は「人」を主語に置くことが多いですが、英語では「物・事」もよく主語になります。

1. **The heavy rain** prevented us from going on a picnic.
   ひどい雨のせいで、私たちはピクニックに行けなかった。

2. **Sport** can help me relieve stress.　スポーツのおかげで、私はストレスを発散できる。

3. **The idea for the event** came from a doctor at the hospital.
   そのイベントを開こうという考えは、その病院のある医師から生まれた。

4. **What I can do** is leave a message for her.　僕ができることは、彼女に伝言を残すことだ。

   ▶ 1から3では、「物」が主語に来て、4では「事」が主語に来ています。
   ▶ 日本語では人が主語に来る文でも、英語では物を主語に置いて表せます（1 2）。

❷ 「人・団体」が主語に来る例 🎧 DL 07 💿 CD07

5. **People** know that the Olympic Games began in Ancient Greece.
   人々はオリンピックが古代ギリシャで始まったことを知っている。

6. Unfortunately, **no one** came to the event.　残念ながら、そのイベントに誰も来なかった。

7. **The Stoke Mandeville Hospital** held a competition for its patients.
   ストーク・マンデビル病院が患者のために競技を開催した。

   ▶ 人や団体名（社名、組織名など）もよく主語に来る要素です。
   ▶ 6の no one（誰も〜ない）のように、否定を示す語句で文を始めることもできます。

❸ 形式的に置かれる it, there 🎧 DL 08 💿 CD08

英語は必ず主語を必要とします。日本語では主語を省く場合でも、主語を置かなければなりません。よって、英語では意味を持たない it や there を主語の位置に置くことがあります。

8. **It** sometimes rains after **it** snows.　雪のあとには時々雨が降る。

9. **It** seems that Katie loves chocolate.　ケイティーはチョコレートが大好きなようだ。

10. Wouldn't **it** be nice if all people were born healthy?　皆が健康に生まれてくるなら、よくないだろうか。

    ▶ 天候について述べるときに it が用いられます（8）。
    ▶ 9と10では、意味を持たない it が主語の位置に置かれています。

11. **There** would be no need for the Paralympic Games at all.
    パラリンピックの試合はまったく必要なくなるだろう。

12. **There** must be easier ways to lose weight.　痩せるにはもっと簡単な方法があるはずだ。

    ▶ 「〜がある、いる」ことを示す there is/are 構文では be 動詞の後に初めて話題に出すものが現れます。

Unit 2　A Reasonable Dream…

Step 1 *Grammar Practice*

以下の英文の（　）には主語が入ります。文中の要素を手掛かりにして、適切な主語を選択肢から選びましょう。

1. Unfortunately, (　　　　　　　　) came to the party yesterday.
2. (　　　　　　　　) helped me a lot. I appreciate it.
3. (　　　　　　　　) has caused a heavy traffic jam on Route 153.
4. (　　　　　　　　) are still some seats available on the plane.
5. Suddenly (　　　　　　　　) came to me.

> a car crash　　there　　no one
> your suggestion　　a new idea

 Step 2 *Create Sentences*

日本語の意味に合わせて、（　）内の語句を並べ替えましょう。

1. 事態がどのようになるか、しばらく見守ろう。
   (see / and / let's / things / go / wait / how).

   _____

2. その著者の新しい本は、私たちに日本経済について異なる視点を与えてくれる。
   (new / the author's / us / the / view / Japanese economy / book / different / a / on / gives).

   _____

3. エンジンに何か問題があるようだ。
   (problem / engine / there / to / the / seems / with / be / a).

   _____

4. 残念ながら、彼がしたことはまったくの間違いでした。
   (wrong / did / he / was / what / unfortunately / totally / ,).

   _____

5. 毎年だいたいこの時期はずいぶん早い時間に暗くなると聞いています。
   (gets / that / it / hear / of / very early / dark / around / I / this time) the year.

   _____

Step 3 Try Writing

日本語の意味に合わせて、[　]内の語句を使って英文にしましょう。

1. 彼女の新しい本は発売直後に注目を集めました。[gained]

_____

2. 次の会議は水曜日に行われます。[take place]

_____

3. コミュニケーション不足のように思います。[seem, lack]

_____

4. この写真を見ると、いつも高校時代を思い出します。[remind]

_____

5. この道を行けば駅に着きますよ。[lead]

_____

Step 4 Write about Yourself

本文の8〜9行目 "He strongly believed that sport could assist the rehabilitation of his patients and help them develop physical strength." のように、あなたが役立つと信じていることについて、本文と以下の例を参考に、英語で短い文章を書いてみましょう。

> 例1 I believe that reading in English helps me improve my English. I make it a rule to read three books a week.
>
> 例2 I believe that regular exercise helps me keep fit, so I run in my local park for thirty minutes every morning.

Unit 3 Japan's Popular Wave

■▶ 時制

Model Essay 太字の表現に注意して読みましょう。

Have you ever **seen** a famous piece of art on the wall of a street? Probably not, as such works **are**, of course, **kept** in art museums. For instance, the home of Leonardo da Vinci's *The Mona Lisa* **is** the Louvre Museum in Paris. It **has been displayed** there for over 200 years. Vincent Van Gogh's *Starry Night*, another well-known masterpiece, **has had** a permanent home in New York's Museum of Modern Art since 1941.

Compared to these works from Europe, *The Great Wave* by the Japanese artist Katsushika Hokusai **is** perhaps even more famous. Hokusai **created** the picture in 1831. Since then, it **has** apparently **been reproduced** more than any other image in the world. In part, the reason **is** that it **is created** from a woodblock, meaning many original prints **can be made**.

Like other famous works of art, *The Great Wave* **is displayed** in museums around the world. Even the great French painter Claude Monet **admired** the work of Hokusai so much that he **put** a copy in his home. However, fans of the wave **have created** new versions. In cities around the world, large murals based on the image **have been painted** on the exterior walls of buildings. Hokusai **must be** happy. Rather than seeing it as graffiti, the locals **admire** the picture's simple but impressive power.

A street mural of Katsushika Hokusai's woodblock classic, *The Great Wave*, features on a wall in Sydney

Notes

masterpiece 傑作、名作   permanent home 永住の地   New York's Museum of Modern Art ニューヨーク近代美術館（正式名称は the Museum of Modern Art で、MoMA [モマ] という略称で親しまれている）   *The Great Wave*「神奈川沖浪裏」（葛飾北斎の浮世絵『富嶽三十六景』の図の一つ）   apparently どうやら〜らしい   reproduce 模写する   woodblock 板目木版画   original print 原画   display 展示する   admire 称賛する、高く評価する   mural 壁画   exterior wall 外壁   graffiti 落書き   the locals 地元民

Grammar for Writing! 時制

❶ 現在形と進行形　　🎧 DL 10　💿 CD 10

現在形は事実や真理、習慣を、現在進行形は今まさに行われている動作を表します。

① These images **are created** from a woodblock.　これらの絵は版画から作られる。
② He **is creating** a beautiful piece of pottery now.　彼は今美しい陶器を製作中である。
▶ ①の現在形は時や状況に左右されない事実を、②は現在進行している動作を表します。

❷ 過去形と現在完了形　　🎧 DL 11　💿 CD 11

過去の出来事を完結した事柄と見なす場合は「過去形」を、出来事が今の時点まで関わりがあると見なす場合は「現在完了形」を用います。過去形は「点」、現在完了形は「帯」のイメージです。

③ Hokusai **created** the picture in 1831.　北斎は1831年にその絵を創作した。
④ Since then, it **has been reproduced** more than any other image in the world.
　　　　　　　　　　　　　　　それ以来、その絵は世界で一番模写されてきた。
▶ ③は1831年に絵を創作したという過去の1つの出来事を述べているのに対し、④は世界中で模写されてきて今日に至るという、これまでの様子を振り返る様子が読み取れます。

⑤ I **used to live** in Osaka, so I'm familiar with the local food there.
　　　　　　　　　　　　　以前大阪に住んでいたので、大阪の食べ物に詳しいですよ。
▶ used to do を用いると、過去に一定期間経験があり、今はしていないことを示します。

❸ 現在完了形を使った様々な表現　　🎧 DL 12　💿 CD 12

⑥ **Have you** ever **seen** a famous piece of art on the wall of a street?
　　　　　　　　　　　　　通りの壁に描かれた有名な芸術作品を見たことがありますか。
⑦ I **have been** to the post office today.　今日郵便局に行ってきたところだ。
▶ ⑥は ever を付けることで、「これまでに~」という経験を尋ねています。
▶ ⑦は過去形でなく完了形を使い、「~したところ」という事実の余韻を残す言い方です。

❹ 過去形と過去完了形　　🎧 DL 13　💿 CD 13

過去完了形は、過去に起こった複数の出来事の時間差を表すことができます。

⑧ The train **had** already **left** when we arrived at the station.
　　　　　　　　　　　　　　駅に着いたときには、もう電車は出てしまっていた。
⑨ I **had** already **finished** the exam before the teacher said "Stop writing, please."
　　　　　　　先生が「解答をやめてください」と言う前に、私はすでに試験を終えていた。
⑩ I **worked** in a library for 30 years and **retired** in 2017.
　　　　　　　　　　　　　　図書館に30年間勤めて、2017年に定年退職した。
▶ ⑧・⑨では下線部の行為より前に主節の出来事があったことを強調しています。
▶ 順序を明示する必要がないときは、⑩のように過去形を続けて用います。

Unit 3　Japan's Popular Wave

Step 1 *Grammar Practice*

以下の英文の（　）には述語が入ります。文中の要素を手掛かりにして、適切な述語を選択肢から選びましょう。

1. I (   ) writing my report and feel relieved now.
2. I (   ) to Brazil many times, but I still don't speak Portuguese.
3. I (   ) the letter before I was told to do so.
4. I (   ) to a bookstore and chose some books as her birthday present.
5. This jacket is exactly the one I (   ).

| have been looking for | had already posted |
| went | have been | have just finished |

 Step 2 *Create Sentences*

日本語の意味に合わせて、（　）内の語句を並べ替えましょう。

1. 息子はまだ学校から帰って来ていません。
   (school / yet / come / my son / hasn't / home / from).
   _____

2. ドイツ語を以前学んでいましたが、今は中国語を勉強しています。
   (study / used / but / I / now / German / Chinese / study / I / to / ,).
   _____

3. 先週渡したハンドアウトを持ってきましたか。
   (bring / did / handout / I / the / last week / you / gave / you)?
   _____

4. ここ4年で、彼の家の価値は2倍になりました。
   (the value / doubled / last / has / of / four years / his house / in / the).
   _____

5. 彼らが到着したときには、私たちはもうすでに料理を始めていました。
   (cooking / already / they / arrived / started / had / we / when / ,).
   _____

Step 3 Try Writing

日本語の意味に合わせて、[　　]内の語句を使って英文にしましょう。

1. IoT（モノのインターネット）について聞いたことがありますか。[hear, the IoT]

2. このあたりのどこかで財布を落としました。[wallet]

3. あの家はずいぶん長い間空き家です。[empty]

4. どちらの授業を取ればよいか、まだ決めかねています。[class]

5. 電車でよく眠れなかったので、パリに着いたときにはとても疲れていました。
[tired, when, because]

Step 4 Write about Yourself

本文の9～10行目 "Since then, it has apparently been reproduced more than any other image in the world." のように、これまで行われてきていること、あるいはあなたがこれまで行ってきたことを、本文と以下の例を参考に、英語で短い文章を書いてみましょう。

> 例1 The new shopping mall in my town has attracted many customers since its opening last month. I definitely want to go there this weekend.
>
> 例2 I have worked on my report for two weeks. Now I am glad it is finished.

Unit 4 Color Matters

▶ 形容詞・副詞

Model Essay   太字の表現に注意して読みましょう。   DL 14   CD 14

　New words **constantly** appear in **most** languages. **Usually**, they are not **controversial**, but **sometimes** how they are represented is. A **good** example is the *emoji*, and a **popular** one **today** is the thumbs-up 'like' symbol. Think about it: how many times have you clicked it **this week** or **this month**? Think
5 **again**, what color was the hand?

　Color matters since social media users come from **different** racial groups. **Naturally**, it follows that choice of skin color is **important**. However, until 2015, when a **black** or a **Latino** person wanted to text a friend the thumbs-up *emoji* via the Internet, a **white** hand was their **only** choice. Now that has
10 changed. A **default** yellow hand appears and it can be altered to one of five skin tones, ranging from "**pale** white" to "**darkest** brown."

　After the color options were introduced, **most non-white** users of Twitter and Facebook **immediately** used them, welcoming the freedom to express their **racial** identity. Yet, this trend has not been taken up so **readily**
15 by **white** people. It seems they feel **uncomfortable** using the **pale** white skin color, believing it may seem to reflect a sense of **high** pride in being **white**. However, whatever color our skin is, shouldn't we be **proud** of it?

Notes

constantly 絶え間なく　　controversial 議論の的となる　　racial group 人種　　naturally 当然
Latino ラテンアメリカ人の　　text（携帯電話で）メールを送る　　default 既定の　　alter（部分的に）変える
range from A to B AからBに及ぶ　　pale 淡い　　immediately すぐに、即座に　　identity 独自性、個性　　take up ～を支持する　　readily すぐに　　uncomfortable 不快な、心地よくない　　reflect 反映する

Grammar for Writing! 　形容詞・副詞

❶ 形容詞の限定用法と叙述用法　　　🎧 DL 15　💿 CD15

名詞の前に置いて使う「限定用法」と、文の補語として使う「叙述用法」を学びましょう。

1. A **good** example is the *emoji*, and a **popular** one today is the thumbs-up 'like' symbol.　よい例が絵文字で、今日人気のあるものは親指を上へ向けた「いいね」のサインだ。
2. Heather is the **only** person in this neighborhood who can speak Swahili.
　　ヘザーがこの界隈でスワヒリ語を話せる唯一の人だ。
3. All the windows were **open**.　窓はすべて開いていた。
4. White people felt **uncomfortable** using the *emoji*.
　　白人の人々はその絵文字を使うのを心地よく感じていなかった。

▶ 限定用法：形容詞を名詞の前に置き、名詞の特性を説明します（1 2）。
▶ 叙述用法：形容詞を動詞の後の補語の位置に置き、名詞の一時的な特性を説明します（3 4）。

5. There is something **wrong** with the computer.　コンピュータに何か不具合がある。

▶ 代名詞 something, anything, nothing の場合は、これらの後に形容詞を置きます。

6. It happened in a **certain** town.　それはある町で起こった。〈限定用法〉
7. He is **certain** to come.　彼はきっと来る。〈叙述用法〉

▶ 限定用法と叙述用法で意味が変わるものもあります。

❷ 形容詞の注意すべき用法　　　🎧 DL 16　💿 CD16

8. The band consists of **six charming Canadian** girls.
　　そのバンドはかわいらしいカナダ人の少女6人で構成される。
9. It is [× I am] **impossible** for me to get there today.　そこに今日行くのは不可能だ。

▶ 複数続く形容詞は、一般的に「冠詞＋序数＋数量＋性状＋大小＋新旧＋色＋材料・所属」の順に並べます（8）。
▶ 形容詞の中には、主語に置く要素に注意が必要なものもあります（9）。

❸ 副詞が修飾するもの　　　🎧 DL 17　💿 CD17

副詞は動詞や形容詞のほか、副詞や接続詞、あるいは文全体を修飾する場合もあります。

10. New words **constantly** appear in most languages.
　　ほとんどの言語で、新しい語が絶え間なく生じる。〈動詞を修飾〉
11. I'm **pretty** sure she will say yes.
　　彼女は「いいよ」と言うだろうと、私はかなり確信している。〈形容詞を修飾〉
12. This trend was not taken up **so** readily by white people.
　　このトレンドは白人にはそれほどすぐに支持されなかった。〈副詞を修飾〉
13. **Naturally,** it follows that choice of skin color is important.
　　当然、皮膚の色の選択が重要になってくる。〈文を修飾〉

Unit 4　Color Matters

Step 1　Grammar Practice

以下の英文の(　)には形容詞または副詞が入ります。文中の要素を手掛かりにして、適切な語を選択肢から選びましょう。

1. It seems (　　　　　) that I was mistaken.
2. My boyfriend always listens to me. I feel (　　　　　) when I speak with him.
3. (　　　　　) enough, George said no to my suggestion this time.
4. This is the (　　　　　) book I've been looking for. This has been out of print for ages.
5. This book is (　　　　　) difficult. I have to check a dictionary again and again while reading it.

strangely	very	clear
pretty	comfortable	

 Step 2　Create Sentences

日本語の意味に合わせて、(　)内の語句を並べ替えましょう。

1. 冷たい飲み物はいかがですか。
   (something / you / would / drink / to / cold / like)?

2. 死刑は国によってはたいへん議論の的になっている問題です。
   (the / highly / a / death penalty / topic / controversial / is) in some countries.

3. エリックは親切にも私を駅まで連れていってくれました。
   (enough / me / Eric / the station / to / kind / was / take / to).

4. そのレストランの料理はかなりよかったです。
   (restaurant / the / was / good / the / food / quite / at).

5. ワインはどれもあまり好きではないのですが、これはとてもおいしいです。
   (very / like / don't / I / good / most / but / is / this / wines / ,).

Step 3 Try Writing

日本語の意味に合わせて、[　]内の語句を使って英文にしましょう。

1. 今日が彼女の誕生日であることをもう少しで忘れるところでした。[almost]

2. このEメールにすぐ返事をください。[immediately]

3. いつがご都合よろしいでしょうか。[convenient, you]

4. 誰かからお金を借りるのは気が引ける。[uncomfortable]

5. ファッションのトレンドはしょっちゅう変わるので、いつも雑誌をチェックしています。[constantly]

Step 4 Write about Yourself

本文の17行目 "However, whatever color our skin is, shouldn't we be proud of it?" にある形容詞 proud を使って、あなたが誇りに思っていることについて、本文と以下の例を参考に、英語で短い文章を書いてみましょう。

> 例1 I feel proud of my father's efforts. He was transferred to the Shanghai office two years ago and started learning Chinese. Now he is a fluent speaker of Chinese.
>
> 例2 I'm very proud to have done some volunteer work last year. Now I realize the importance of helping others.

Unit 5 Business, Not Bullets
▶ 名詞

Model Essay 太字の表現に注意して読みましょう。   DL 18   CD 18

　Stories connected with **war** do not usually have happy **endings**, but there are **exceptions**. After the September 11th 2001 terrorist **attacks** in New York, many US **soldiers** were sent to fight in Afghanistan. After serving there, one **soldier**, Matthew Griffin, decided to quit the **military** and help promote
5 **peace** in **countries** affected by war and **poverty**. For him, that meant creating **jobs** in such **places**.

　In 2009, during a personal **visit** to Afghanistan, Mr. Griffin suddenly had an **idea** related to **footwear**. He noticed that **flip-flops** were popular there, so two **years** later he launched a **business** to manufacture them. His idea was to
10 sell the Afghan-made flip-flops to **the US** and other countries. Unfortunately, it was not possible to make them in Afghanistan, but Griffin did not give up on his idea. Currently, his company's flip-flops are all made in Columbia, and provide much needed **jobs** for poor **locals** there.

　Back in Afghanistan, **women** in his company make **products** such as
15 **sarongs** and **scarves**. And for any and every **item** his company sells, 10% of the **profit** is put toward building **schools** and educating poor **people** in Afghanistan, especially **girls**. The company also gathers **donations** for clearing **landmines** in **Laos** and providing **healthcare** and medical **training** in countries that
20 desperately need them.

　The happy ending to this **story** can be seen in Mr. Griffin's **company motto**: "Business, Not Bullets."

Notes

exception 例外　　terrorist テロリスト　　military 軍隊　　poverty 貧困、貧乏　　footwear 履物
flip-flop ビーチサンダル　　launch 開始する　　give up on 見切りをつける　　product 製品　　sarong サロン（腰に巻きつけてはくスカート状の服）　　scarf スカーフ、マフラー　　item 品物　　profit 利益、儲け
put A toward B AをBの費用に充てる　　donation 寄付　　landmine 地雷　　healthcare 医療
desperately 本気で　　bullet 銃弾

Grammar for Writing! 名詞

❶ 可算名詞と不可算名詞

英語には、数えることができる「可算名詞」と数えられない「不可算名詞」があります。

可算名詞	普通名詞	dictionary, lawyer, place など
	集合名詞	class, audience, professional など
不可算名詞	物質名詞	water, bread, wood, furniture など
	抽象名詞	beauty, information, poverty など
	固有名詞	Halloween, Stanford University, Afghanistan など

❷ 普通名詞と集合名詞

1. I love **dogs**, but I got **a cat** from my cousin yesterday.
   私はイヌ好きだが、昨日いとこからネコを一匹もらった。

   ▶ 普通名詞：①では特定のイヌでなく種全体を示しているため、複数形の dogs を用います。a cat の冠詞 a は、「もらったネコ以外にも（世の中には）存在する」ことを示唆します。

2. The **committee** has rejected the proposal. その委員会はその提案に反対している。

3. The **crew** were injured and taken to the hospital.
   乗組員は（みな）負傷し、その病院へ運ばれた。

4. The **police** are searching the neighborhood. 警察が近所を捜索している。

   ▶ 集合名詞：全体を1つのまとまりと捉える場合は単数として（②）、成員一人一人を意識する場合は複数として扱います（③）。ただし the police のように常に複数扱いする集合名詞もあります（④）。

❸ 物質名詞と抽象名詞

5. She took out a piece of **paper** and wrote down her e-mail address.
   彼女は一枚の紙を取り出し、Eメールアドレスを書き記した。

6. I eat two slices of **toast** every morning. 私は毎朝、トーストを二枚食べる。

   ▶ 物質名詞：不可算名詞として用いますが、単位を付けることで、単数や複数の概念を表せます。

7. **Science** reveals why **breakfast** is important for us.
   朝食がなぜ我々にとってなぜ大事なのか、科学が明らかにしている。

8. He gave me a good piece of **information**. 彼が私によい情報をくれた。

9. They suffer from **war** and **poverty** every day. 彼らは毎日戦争と貧困に喘いでいる。

10. **A terrible war** occurred between the two countries.
    二国間で凄まじい戦争が起こった。 ※特定の戦争を指す場合は a [the] war となる。

    ▶ 抽象名詞：基本的には不可算名詞として用いますが（⑦）、information などの抽象名詞は a piece of / ～ pieces of を付けて単数や複数の概念を表すこともできます（⑧）。

    ▶ war のように抽象名詞と普通名詞の両方があるもの（⑨ ⑩）は、意味によって a が付くことがあります。

Unit 5 Business, Not Bullets

Step 1 Grammar Practice

以下の英文には誤りがあります。直すべき 1 語に○を付け、正しい形にして空所に書き入れましょう。

1. You should take medicines to lower your fever. → 正 [   ]
2. Is this your first visiting to New Zealand? → 正 [   ]
3. How many pieces of baggages do you have? → 正 [   ]
4. I think his opinion is of great important. → 正 [   ]
5. Statistic is my favorite subject. I always get full marks in those tests.
   → 正 [   ]

 Step 2 Create Sentences

日本語の意味に合わせて、(　　) 内の語句を並べ替えましょう。

1. 今年、スタッフはみなよい仕事をしました。
   (entire / has / the / staff / a / job / great / this year / done).

   _____

2. そのレストランは地元の人のお気に入りですが、観光客の間ではあまり知られていません。
   (among visitors / is / the restaurant / it / by locals / loved / well known / not / is / so / but /,).

   _____
   _____

3. まだ仕事がたくさん残っているので、帰ることができません。
   (still / work / I / leave / have / can't / I / now / so / a lot of / ,).

   _____

4. 研究によって、牛乳が好きな人は長生きすると示されています。
   (lovers / longer / shows / live / milk / that / research).

   _____

5. その会議の聴衆は、彼女のスピーチに感動しました。
   (impressed / conference / audience / was / the / the / at) by her speech.

   _____

Step 3 Try Writing

日本語の意味に合わせて、[   ]内の語句を使って英文にしましょう。

1. 私はサンドイッチよりピザのほうが好きです。[prefer]

   _____

2. 私は先生から2つ助言をもらいました。[advice]

   _____

3. お水をいただけますか。[Could I]

   _____

4. 私の学校は地元のある企業から、多額の寄付を得ました。[local company]

   _____

5. 川にかかっている橋は鉄でできています。[made of]

   _____

Step 4 Write about Yourself

本文の9行目 "he launched a business to manufacture them" のように、あなたがやりたい（架空の）仕事について、本文と以下の例を参考に、英語で短い文章を書いてみましょう。

> 例1 I would like to launch a business to sell my local tea on the Internet. I believe that it is the most delicious tea that I've ever tasted.
>
> 例2 I would like to launch a business to find good books for customers. Based on the data of their age and lifestyles, I would look for the ones that suit their preferences.

Unit 6 Spices for Life!

冠詞・数量詞

Model Essay 太字の表現に注意して読みましょう。   DL 22   CD22

India is **an** exotic country with **a** diverse mixture of ethnicities. This diversity is reflected in its most famous dish, curry. And with **hundreds of** varieties to suit different tastes, are there **any** people who dislike it? Actually, curry may be **one** of the world's most favorite meals. It may also be **one** of the world's healthiest meals.

Research suggests that **the** spices found in curries may help prevent **some** major illnesses. **An** example is Alzheimer's disease (loss of memory), which is **a** growing concern in **many** countries. But scientists at **the** University of California reported that turmeric, **a** spice used in **the** majority of curries, contains **a** chemical that counters **the** disease and may even improve memory. Turmeric also has **the** power to fight infection, maintain strong bones and reduce **the** possibility of cancer. Also, **the** spices cardamom and sweet basil are said to reduce blood pressure and thus prevent heart attacks.

This is good news for **a lot of** Japanese people. Even though Japanese curry may contain **few** spices when compared with **most** curries in India, it is **one** of **the** nation's most popular dishes. In fact, **the** government reported that on average, **each** Japanese person eats curry and rice at least once **a** week. Such popularity should help to keep **the** nation **a little** healthier!

Notes

exotic 異国情緒あふれる　　diverse 多様な　　ethnicity 民族性　　variety 種類、変種　　Alzheimer's disease アルツハイマー病　　concern 懸念、心配　　turmeric ターメリック（ウコンの地下茎を乾燥した香辛料）　　majority 大多数　　chemical 化学物質　　counter 抑制する　　infection 感染症、伝染病　　reduce 減らす　　cancer 癌　　cardamom カルダモン　　basil バジル　　blood pressure 血圧　　heart attack 心臓発作、心臓麻痺

Grammar for Writing! 冠詞・数量詞

❶ 冠詞　　DL 23　CD23

冠詞には、新たに話題に上った事柄や特定されない名詞に付く不定冠詞（a / an）と、状況によってそれとわかるものに付く定冠詞（the）があります。

1. India is **an** exotic country. I visited **the** country last year.
   インドは異国情緒豊かな国だ。私はその国を昨年訪れた。
2. **The** earth goes around **the** sun. 地球は太陽の周りをまわる。
3. Turmeric has **the** power to fight infection. ターメリックには感染症と戦う力がある。

- ▶ 不定冠詞 a / an：数あるもののうちの1つであることを示します（①はインドが世界に数ある exotic countries の一国であるとわかる）。
- ▶ 定冠詞 the：前に出てきた名詞や文脈からそれとわかるもの（①）、唯一のもの（②）に付きます。また、抽象的な名詞の後ろに of... などの前置詞句や to 不定詞が置かれてより具体性が高まったときに、the が付きやすくなります（③）。

4. I commute to **school** by **bus**. バスで通学している。

- ▶ 無冠詞：可算名詞を単数形で冠詞を付けずに使う場合、その「機能」に焦点が当たります（④）。

❷ 不定の数量を表す数量詞　　DL 24　CD24

「1つ、2つ」と具体的な数量ではなく、「多くの、いくつかの」といった不定の数量を表す語句があります。

5. Japanese curry contains **few** spices. 日本のカレーにはスパイスがほとんど含まれない。
6. This is good news for **a lot of** people. これは多くの人々にとってよい知らせだ。
7. On average, **each** Japanese person eats curry and rice once a month.
   平均して、日本人はそれぞれカレーライスを月に一度は食べる。

- ▶ few は可算名詞，little は不可算名詞に付いて「ほとんどない」という意味を表します（a が付くと「少しある」になる）。
- ▶ a lot of「たくさんの」は可算名詞にも不可算名詞にも使うことができます。
- ▶ each / every はあとに単数形の可算名詞がきます（each は代名詞の用法もあります）。

8. Can I have **some** water?（少し）水をもらえますか。
9. Are there [Do you have] **any** questions? 何か質問ありますか。
10. You can take **any** bread here. ここにあるどのパンを持って行ってもいいですよ。

- ▶ some は一定のものが想定されている場合に使います（⑧では some によって「少しいただけますか」とやや丁寧なニュアンスが加わる）。一方 any は一定の数を想定せず、「あるかもしれないし、ないかもしれない」という意識があります（⑨）。
- ▶ any＋単数名詞で「どんな〜でも」という意味になります（⑩）。

Unit 6　Spices for Life!

Step 1 *Grammar Practice*

以下の英文の（　）に冠詞あるいは数量詞を入れましょう。何も入れる必要がない場合は、×を書き入れましょう。

1. Would you like to pay in (　　　) cash or by (　　　) credit card?
2. First, stir-fry the beef and onion for five minutes in a pan. Then add (　　　) remaining ingredients and mix together well.
3. The books on the top shelf are mine. (　　　) others are all my father's.
4. I'll give you (　　　) ride to the station.
5. Good poems remind us of (　　　) power of language.

 Step 2 *Create Sentences*

日本語の意味に合わせて、（　）内の語句を並べ替えましょう。

1. 残念ながら、あなたにお伝えすべきよくない知らせがあります。
   (afraid / some / have / to / I'm / you / news / I / tell / bad).

2. ここにいる学生はほとんど英語を専攻しています。
   (majors / all / here / English / almost / the / of / students / are).

3. あなたの予想どおり、彼らは再度彼女を社長に選びました。
   (you / president / they / as / her / expected / elected / ,) again.

4. このクラスの学生はみな、一生懸命勉強します。
   (hard / student / works / this / in / every / class / really).

5. 近ごろスパムメールがよく届きますが、私たちは昨日30分ほどその件について話しました。
   We get lots of spam e-mails these days and (discussed / hour / we / for / the / about / half / matter / an / yesterday).

Step 3 Try Writing

日本語の意味に合わせて、[　]内の語句を使って英文にしましょう。[　]内の語句は形が変わる場合があります。

1. 私はほぼ毎日アイスクリームを食べています。[ice cream]

2. ボストンでは、我々はいたるところでリスを見ます。[squirrel]

3. 私は今お金がほんの少ししかないので、アルバイトを探さないといけない。
　　　　　　　　　　　　　　　　　　　　　　　　[money, a part-time job]

4. 少なくとも、1日に2回は歯を磨くべきだ。[tooth]

5. 我が社は新たな企画を検討中です。どんな提案も歓迎します。[suggestions]

Step 4 Write about Yourself

本文の1行目 "India is an exotic country with a diverse mixture of ethnicities." のように、あなたが紹介したい国や町などの魅力について、本文と以下の例を参考に、英語で短い文章を書いてみましょう。(名詞を用いる際には冠詞と数量詞に注意しましょう。)

> 例1　Nagoya is an interesting city with lots of delicious local food. Among them, I love *misokatsu*, which is pork cutlet with miso sauce.
>
> 例2　Hungary is a wonderful country with a traditional atmosphere. You can see lots of historical buildings and enjoy hot springs there.

Unit 6 Spices for Life!

Unit 7 Plastic Planet

■▶ 分詞

Model Essay 太字の表現に注意して読みましょう。 DL 25 CD 25

Approximately 150 years ago, plastic did not exist on Earth. Today, however, imagining life without this adaptable man-made material is impossible. Although it has made our lives easier in various ways, its creation has also brought an **unwanted** side effect.

Recent news reports have highlighted the volume of plastic **floating** in the world's seas and oceans. Even in exotic locations, like the island of Bali in Indonesia, there is a **mounting** trash problem **caused** by this **manufactured** material. **Determined** to solve the problem on the island, two young sisters decided to take action.

In 2013, 10- and 13-year-old Melati and Isabel Wijsen started a campaign **called** "Bye Bye Plastic Bags." They wanted a new law **banning** these items completely, and to achieve their goal, they engaged in various activities such as cleaning local beaches. Also, they asked the public to sign a petition, **obtaining** over 100,000 signatures.

Noting the sisters' hard work and public support, the governor of Bali decided to ban plastic bags on the island by 2018. This big success by two little girls is great news, but action is required on a global scale. According to the Earth Policy Institute, each year, we use 1,000,000,000,000 plastic bags worldwide, or 2 million every minute. Clearly, our planet needs many more **caring** individuals like Melati and Isabel.

Melati and Isabel Wijsen pose after receiving the 2017 Bambi Award in the "Our Earth" category

Notes

approximately おおよそ、約　　adaptable 機能的な、適応できる　　creation 創作、開発　　side effect 副作用　　highlight 強調する　　float 浮く　　the island of Bali バリ島　　mount 増加する　　trash ごみ　　engage in 〜に従事する　　petition 嘆願書　　obtain 得る　　signature 署名　　note 気づく　　the governor of Bali バリ島総督　　Earth Policy Institute アースポリシー研究所（アメリカの非営利環境保護団体）

Grammar for Writing! 分詞

❶ 名詞を修飾する分詞（形容詞的用法） 🎧 DL 26 💿 CD 26

分詞には、現在分詞形（-ing）と、過去分詞形（-ed）があります。

1. The **growing** company achieved its highest sales last year.
   その成長している企業は昨年、最高の売上高を達成した。
2. Some **excited** fans stayed late at the stadium.
   興奮したファンが遅くまで球場に残っていた。
3. The news reports highlighted the plastic **floating** in the sea.
   そのニュース報道は、海に浮かんでいるプラスチックに焦点を当てていた。
4. I joined the party **held** at John's place. 私はジョンの家で行われたパーティに参加した。

   ▶ 分詞：単独のときは修飾する名詞の前（1 2）、他の語句を伴うときは後（3 4）に置きます。
   ▶ 現在分詞：修飾する名詞と分詞が能動態の関係の場合（1 3）に用いられます。
   ▶ 過去分詞：修飾する名詞と分詞が受動態の関係の場合（2 4）に用いられます。

❷ 補語になる分詞 🎧 DL 27 💿 CD 27

SVC や SVOC の形の構文では、C の位置に分詞を用いて動詞の意味を補完するものがあります。

5. The girl on stage kept **crying**. 舞台の上の女の子はずっと泣いていた。
6. Tax rates have remained **unchanged** for years. 税率は何年も変わっていない。
7. I found my teacher **reading** a thick book in the library.
   私は先生が図書館で分厚い本を読んでいるのに気づいた。
8. Don't leave your homework **undone**. 宿題をほったらかしにしてはいけません。
9. I can't concentrate on my work **with this noise going on**.
   この騒音が続く状態では、仕事に集中できない。

   ▶ 分詞は補語としても使われます。5〜8 は動詞だけでは意味が完結せず、補語を必要とします。SVOC では O と C が〈主語＋動詞〉のような関係になります（7 8）。
   ▶ with 〜 … の形で、「〜が…の状況で」という付帯状況を示します（9）。

❸ 副詞の働きをする分詞（分詞構文） 🎧 DL 28 💿 CD 28

分詞で始まる句が副詞の働きをする分詞構文の用法を見てみましょう。

10. **Noting** their hard work, the governor decided to ban plastic bags.
    彼女たちの熱心な仕事に気づき、総督はレジ袋を禁止することを決めた。
11. **Determined** to solve the problem, they took action.
    その問題を解決しようと決心して、彼女たちは行動を起こした。
12. I studied Turkish for one year **while working** full-time.
    常勤で働きながら、1年間トルコ語を勉強した。

    ▶ 分詞構文は接続詞の意味を持ちますが、12 のように接続詞が残り〈接続詞＋分詞構文〉の形になることもあります。

Unit 7 **Plastic Planet**

Step 1 Grammar Practice

以下の英文の末尾に [ ] で示した語を適切な分詞にして、(   ) に書き入れましょう。

1. J. K. Rowling is a British writer (   ) for her *Harry Potter* series. [know]
2. This article will tell you how to deal with (   ) neighbors. [annoy]
3. TV commercials (   ) at young children are sometimes controversial. [target]
4. His latest book is quite useful for those (   ) in computer science. [interest]
5. Humans emit carbon dioxide in a variety of ways, (   ) climate change all over the world. [cause]

Step 2 Create Sentences

日本語の意味に合わせて、(   ) 内の語句を並べ替えましょう。

1. 平易な英語で書かれているので、彼女の小説は読みやすい。
   (simple / in / read / her / written / to / English / novel / easy / is / ,).
   _____

2. 郵便で届いた小包には、子どもへの誕生日プレゼントが入っていました。
   The package (the child's / present / postal mail / contained / birthday / by / delivered).
   _____

3. 私は先生がカフェで友だちと話しているのを見つけました。
   (cafe / found / chatting / I / at / my teacher / with / a / her friend).
   _____

4. 2番線に入ってくる電車は、熊本行きです。
   (train / Kumamoto / for / Platform 2 / bound / the / approaching / is).
   _____

5. 腕を組んだまま、人の話を聞いてはいけません。
   (with / listen / folded / someone / your / to / don't / arms).
   _____

Step 3　Try Writing

日本語の意味に合わせて、[　]内の語句を使って英文にしましょう。[　]内の語句は形が変わる場合があります。

1. 舞台で歌っている女性は、私のいとこです。[stage, cousin]
   _____

2. パリに滞在中、私は地元のレストランでおいしい料理をたくさん食べました。
   [while, stay]
   _____

3. スペイン語はこの地域で話されている言語のうちの一つです。[area]
   _____

4. この地域はここ50年何も変わっていません。[unchanged, over]
   _____

5. 医者になると決心して、彼女は毎日夜遅くまで勉強しています。[determined]
   _____

Step 4　Write about Yourself

本文の10～11行目 "Melati and Isabel Wijsen started a campaign called 'Bye Bye Plastic Bags.'" のように、あなたが携わった企画や活動について、本文と以下の例を参考に、英語で短い文章を書いてみましょう。（called を使って企画名を紹介した後、実際の内容を書きましょう。過去に経験がなければ、架空の企画でもかまいません）

> 例1　I worked on a project called "Go Green!" with my classmates in my high school days. We collected pet bottle caps for recycling.
>
> 例2　I'm thinking of making a group called "Talk a Lot" with my classmates. We are planning to meet every Monday evening and talk with each other in English.

Unit 8 London Coffee and Lazy Men

関係詞

Model Essay　太字の表現に注意して読みましょう。

　Coffee is a drink **that** is attracting more and more fans around the world. Even in the UK, **which** is often considered a nation of tea-lovers, this dark drink is experiencing a boom in consumption. For example, like many cities today, London is a place **that** has plenty of cafes on its streets. Interestingly, this situation was not so different in the English capital several centuries ago.

　It was in 1652 that coffee first appeared in London, **where** it was sold from a simple street stall **whose** owner was Greek. The owner was a man named Pasqua Roseé, **who** imported the coffee from Turkey. Soon, Roseé's drink became a hit with Londoners, **to whom** he was selling over 600 cups per day. Others noticed his success, **which** quickly led to coffeehouses springing up all over the city. By 1663, the central area had around eighty cafes, a number **that** grew to over five hundred not many years later.

　The London coffeehouses were businesses **that** saw few female customers. Instead, they served primarily as places **where** men met to discuss various matters. In fact, when visiting the coffeehouses, the men saw it as a time **when** they could conduct business, make important judgments and think of great new ideas. Women, however, saw coffee as an addictive drink and criticized the coffeehouses for making their men lazy!

Notes

attract 引き寄せる　consider 考える、見なす　dark 黒い、濃い　consumption 消費、摂取
plenty of たくさんの〜　situation 状況　capital 首都　Greek ギリシャ人の　Turkey トルコ
spring up 急に現れる　female 女性の　instead その代わりに　serve 役割を果たす　primarily 主に
conduct 行う　judgment 判断　addictive 中毒性の　criticize 批判する　lazy 怠惰な

Grammar for Writing! 関係詞

❶ 関係節とは　　　　　　　　　　　　　　　　　　🎧 DL 30　💿 CD30

関係節は、関係詞を用いて名詞を後ろから修飾し、名詞の意味を深めます。

1. Coffee is <u>a drink</u> **that** is attracting more fans around the world.
   コーヒーは世界中で愛好者を増やし続けている飲み物である。

2. I have <u>some friends</u> **who** I often go camping with. 私にはよくキャンプに行く友人がいる。

3. I got a cup of coffee from <u>a street stall</u> **whose** owner was Greek.
   私はオーナーがギリシャ人の露店でコーヒーを1杯買った。

4. That is not **what** I meant to do. それは私がしようと思ったことではない。

  ▶ 関係代名詞が導く節は、主語（1）、目的語（2）のいずれかが欠けた文になります。欠けている部分には先行詞を補って考えます。
    （例）2では I often go camping with some friends . が成り立つ。
  ▶ 〈関係代名詞 whose ＋名詞〉は〈先行詞 's ＋名詞〉の意味を表します（3）。
  ▶ what は先行詞を含む関係代名詞で、「～すること、もの」という意味です（4）。

❷ 関係副詞　　　　　　　　　　　　　　　　　　🎧 DL 31　💿 CD31

関係副詞は、「前置詞＋関係代名詞」の働きをし、場所・時・理由などを説明します。

5. They served as <u>places</u> **where** men met to discuss various matters.
   それらは男性がさまざまな問題を話し合うために集まる場所としての役割を果たした。

6. I still remember <u>the day</u> **when** I first saw you. 初めて会った日のことをまだ覚えている。

7. I have <u>two reasons</u> **why** I support Bob's idea. ボブの考えを支持する理由が2つある。

  ▶ 関係副詞 where は〈場所〉、when は〈時〉について詳しく説明するときに使います。
  ▶ the reason why ...「～する理由」など、特定の語と結びつく関係副詞もあります（7）。

❸ 関係節の制限用法と非制限用法　　　　　　　　　🎧 DL 32　💿 CD32

関係詞の前にカンマ（,）をつけ、先行詞を付加的に説明する用法を非制限用法と呼びます。
※対して、❶❷の用法は先行詞を「限定」する働きがあるため制限用法と呼ばれます（例1の **a drink that is attracting more fans** の関係節は、数あるうちの「飲み物」を限定）。

8. The owner was a man named <u>Pasqua Roseé</u>, **who** imported the coffee from Turkey. オーナーはパスカ・ロゼという名前の男性で、彼はトルコからコーヒーを輸入した。

9. Coffee first appeared in <u>London</u>, **where** it was sold from a simple street stall.
   コーヒーは初めロンドンに登場し、そこで通りにある普通の売店で売られた。

10. <u>New Yorkers saw his success</u>, **which** led to many *ramen* shops springing up in the city. ニューヨーカーたちが彼の成功を見たことで、街にラーメン店が次々と生まれた。

  ▶ 非制限用法は先行詞を付加的に説明をする働きを持ちます。この用法では，名詞だけでなく、前の節を先行詞とすることもできます（10）。

Unit 8　**London Coffee and Lazy Men**

Step 1　Grammar Practice

以下の英文の（　　）に適切な関係詞を書き入れましょう。

1. I met a great novelist (　　　　　　) books sell well among young ladies.
2. I don't want to hire a person (　　　　　　) cannot use a computer.
3. This is one of the few schools (　　　　　　) Russian is taught to all students.
4. I'll never forget the day (　　　　　　) I first tasted the great local food in Taipei.
5. My boyfriend gave me a letter, (　　　　　　) I read immediately.

Step 2　Create Sentences

日本語の意味に合わせて、（　　）内の語句を並べ替えましょう。

1. ここが私が自転車を買ったお店です。
   (bought / bicycle / this / my / where / the shop / I / is).

2. インターネットでは、今は絶版になっている本を何冊か読むことができます。
   On the Internet, (some / you / print / gone / read / out of / can / books / have / that).

3. 宝くじで1等を取った女性に会いました。
   (who / a lottery / a lady / I / prize / in / won / first / met).

4. ジャマールがテストでよくできたことは、私にとってはかなりの驚きでした。
   (Jamal / me / which / well / surprise / very / did / the test / was / quite a / to / on / ,).

5. 春は多くの新しい花々が芽を出す季節です。
   (appear / the season / many / when / spring / flowers / new / is).

Step 3 Try Writing

日本語の意味に合わせて、[　]内の語句を使って英文にしましょう。[　]内の語句は形が変わる場合があります。

1. おいしい紅茶を出してくれるカフェに連れて行ってあげるよ。[serve]

2. これが私が自分の計画を変えたくない主な理由です。[reason]

3. 私の母は1964年生まれですが、その年は東京オリンピックが開かれた年です。
   [the Tokyo Olympics, hold]

4. 早く帰りたい人は、そのようにしてもらって構いません。[those, leave]

5. これは私がずっと探し求めていたTシャツです。[T-shirt]

Step 4 Write about Yourself

本文の4行目 "London is a place that has plenty of cafes" のように、どこかの都市や町の魅力について、本文と以下の例を参考に、英語で短い文章を書いてみましょう。

> 例1 Kagawa is a place that has plenty of *udon* restaurants. You can eat delicious *Sanuki udon*, which has a firm and chewy texture, at a reasonable price.
>
> 例2 Alaska is a place where we can see beautiful stars and the Northern Lights. I definitely want to go there someday.

Unit 9 Jacques' Lung

▶ 比較

Model Essay　太字の表現に注意して読みましょう。　DL33　CD33

Long ago, sailors often told stories about monsters rising from **the deepest** oceans to attack ships. This led to some fear and much curiosity about what life forms actually live there. But finding out was considered impossible, since humans cannot, of course, breathe under water.

However, one man's passion for protecting marine life was **greater** than anything else. Subsequently, it led him to invent an underwater breathing device, the Aqua-Lung. Jacques Cousteau was a French undersea explorer, photographer and writer. Thanks to his 1942 invention, it became much **easier** than before to observe and appreciate the diversity and beauty of Earth's deep waters.

Strangely, though, the lung's **earliest** usage was not related to marine biology. When World War II ended, it was used in operations to remove remaining mines from French seas. For Cousteau, however, the main purpose of the lung was different. He wanted to create **better** public awareness about the ocean's natural treasures and how pollution destroys them. So, by using the device in his popular TV series *The Undersea World of Jacques Cousteau*, he was able to achieve this.

The United Nations describes the oceans as "the lungs of our planet, providing most of the oxygen we breathe." By inventing the Aqua-Lung, Cousteau's goal was simply to bring them **greater** protection and keep them **as healthy as** possible.

Notes

rise from ～から生じる　curiosity 好奇心　breathe 呼吸する　device 装置　explorer 探検家　appreciate 正しく理解する　diversity 多様性　usage 使用　relate A to B AとBを関連付ける　biology 生物学　operation 業務　remove 取り除く　remaining 残りの　mine 地雷　public awareness 世間一般の認識　pollution 汚染　oxygen 酸素

Grammar for Writing! 比較

❶ 比較級と最上級 🎧 DL 34　💿 CD34

2つ以上のものを比べるとき、形容詞や副詞の比較級・最上級を使います。

1. Humans live **longer** than dogs.　ヒトはイヌよりも長生きする。
2. It has become **much easier** than before to observe **the deepest** oceans.
   深海を観察することが以前よりはるかに容易になった。
3. We should keep the sea **as healthy as** possible.　私たちは海を可能な限り健康に保つべきだ。

   ▶ 比較級：語尾に -er をつけて、「(2つのものを比べて)〜の方が…だ」という意味を表します。
   ▶ 最上級：the + -est をつけて、「(3つ以上のもののうち)〜が最も…だ」という意味を表します。
   ▶ as 〜 as ... :「…と同じくらい〜である」と言うときに使います。

4. **The temperature** in cities is **higher** than **that** in villages.
   都市部の気温は村の気温より高い。
5. I can do it **as well as** you (can).　私はあなたと同じくらい上手にそれができる。
6. I can't do it **as well as** you can.　あなたほど上手に私はそれができない。

   ▶ ④では temperature の繰り返しを避けるために than 以下を that で置き換えています。
   ▶ as や than のあとの be 動詞や代名詞、助動詞は省略することができます (⑤)。ただし、⑥のように、意味の面から助動詞が省略できない場合もあるため、注意が必要です。

❷ 比較・最上級の不規則変化　🎧 DL 35　💿 CD35

比較級・最上級になるとき、不規則に変化する形容詞・副詞があります。

原級	比較級	最上級	原級	比較級	最上級
good / well	better	best	many / much	more	most
bad	worse	worst	little	less	least

7. She has **more** money than she needs.　彼女は必要以上にお金を持っている。
8. She spent **the least** money of all.　全員の中で彼女が最もお金を使わなかった。

❸ 比較級を用いた様々な表現　🎧 DL 36　💿 CD36

9. Healthy food costs **three times as much as** junk food.
   健康的な食べ物は、ジャンクフードの3倍費用がかかる。
10. That mountain is **half as high as** Mt. Fuji.　あの山は富士山の半分の高さだ。
11. **The harder** you work, **the better** the results will be.
    一生懸命勉強すればするほど、よい結果が得られるだろう。
12. His passion for protecting marine life was **greater than anything else**.
    海洋生物を守ろうという彼の情熱は他の何よりも大きいものだった。

    ▶ as 〜 as の前に X times を置き、「〜倍」という意味になります (⑨)。half を置くと、「半分」の意味になります (⑩)。
    ▶ the 比較級 SV 〜, the 比較級 SV ... は「〜すればするほどいっそう…」という意味を表せます (⑪)。

Unit 9　Jacques' Lung

Step 1 Grammar Practice

[   ] 内の語を文脈に合う適切な形にして、(   ) 内に書き入れましょう。

1. I believe that Brian is the (   ) person for this position. [suitable]
2. The sales figures were much (   ) than expected. [good]
3. Restaurant management is not as (   ) as it looks. [easy]
4. The study says that people in Japan take the (   ) amount of vacation time among major advanced countries. [little]
5. Russian is (   ) language I have ever studied. [difficult]

Step 2 Create Sentences

日本語の意味に合わせて、(   ) 内の語句を並べ替えましょう。

1. 我々は今年はこの機械に悩まされることが少なかったです。
   (trouble / this year / had / machine / we've / this / less / with).

   _____

2. 彼の稼ぎは上司の半分です。
   (boss / half / as / earns / he / his / as / much).

   _____

3. 彼女は今年は昨年よりもよりたくさん本を出版しました。
   (she / books / than / published / this year / last year / has / more).

   _____

4. ボストンは今まで行った中で一番すてきな場所のうちの1つです。
   (places / to / one / Boston / that / is / been / of / ever / I / the / have / best).

   _____

5. 私が驚いたことに、彼のスイングは以前よりもはるかによくなっていました。
   (before / my surprise / his swing / become / better / to / than / much / has / ,).

   _____

Step 3 Try Writing

日本語の意味に合わせて、[　]内の語句を使って英文にしましょう。[　]内の語句は形が変わる場合があります。

1. ジョージはすべての男の子の中で一番よくしゃべる男の子です。[talkative]

2. そのカフェはいつもほどには混んでいませんでした。[crowded]

3. ロサンゼルスの気候はニューヨークよりもずっと穏やかです。[climate]

4. 彼女のミスは、彼と同じくらい少なかったです。[make, mistake]

5. あなたが多く話すほど、彼はあなたの話を聞こうとしなくなります。[more, less]

Step 4 Write about Yourself

本文の5～6行目 "one man's passion for protecting marine life was greater than anything else" のように、あなたが他の何よりも大切だと考えていることや、他の誰よりも素晴らしいと考えている人について、本文と以下の例を参考に、英語で短い文章を書いてみましょう。

> 例1 I think that studying English is more important than anything else. In fact, I spend about two hours reading a paperback, watching CNN news and writing my diary every night.
>
> 例2 I believe that Ichiro is greater than any other baseball player. I think his passion and effort inspire a lot of people.

Unit 10 Disease vs. Hunger

➡ 助動詞

Model Essay 太字の表現に注意して読みましょう。

You **may** know the word "malaria," and if you do, you **ought to** know it is one of the world's most serious public health issues. Spread by mosquitoes, it infects around 212 million people every year, with about 90% of all cases occurring in Africa. In fact, this year, too, malaria **will** take the lives of nearly three-quarters of a million African children. If something is not done, more **shall** continue to die. So, how **could** malaria be prevented?

Special bed nets **might** be one simple, effective and inexpensive solution. These nets are treated with chemicals that kill mosquitoes but do not affect humans. Costing only five to ten dollars per net, each one **can** save a life. One organization, Project Mosquito Net, is trying to do this. It has gathered donations and distributed 450 million of the nets in Africa, which has helped cut malaria-related deaths by 50% since 2000.

However, malaria is not the only problem facing people in Africa. Every day, many face the issue of hunger, but they **must** eat. So even though they **should** use the bed nets to protect themselves from mosquito bites, they often sew them together to make large fishing nets. Then they use the nets to catch food. Regarding this practice, one father with a large family said, "I know it's not right but without these nets, we **wouldn't** eat."

Workers demonstrate how to use treated mosquito nets in Afambo, Ethiopia

Notes

malaria マラリア（マラリア原虫を持った蚊から感染する病気）　spread 広める　mosquito 蚊　infect 感染する　nearly ほとんど　effective 効果的な　inexpensive 高価でない　solution 解決策　treat（科学的に）処理する　affect 影響する　organization 組織　distribute 分配する、割り当てる　face 直面する　hunger 飢餓　sew 縫う　regarding 〜に関して

Grammar for Writing! 助動詞

助動詞は、動詞の原形の前に置かれ、動詞だけでは出せない意味を生み出します。

❶ 可能・推量を表す助動詞　🎧 DL 38　💿 CD38

1. This net **can** save a life. この網は命を救うことができる。
2. How **could** malaria be prevented? どうしたらマラリアは防ぎうるだろうか。

▶ can/could は「〜できる」という可能や、「〜しうる」という可能性の意味を持ちます。

3. You **may** know the word "malaria." あなたは「マラリア」という語を知っているかもしれない。
4. You **may** come to the office at 2 p.m. 午後2時にオフィスに来ていただいて構いません。
5. Special bed nets **might** be one simple solution to malaria. 特別な蚊帳がマラリアに対するシンプルな解法になるかもしれない。

▶ may は「〜かもしれない」(推量)や、「〜してもよい」(許可)を表します。might も推量の意味を持ちます。

6. This year, too, malaria **will** take the lives of many African children. 今年もまたマラリアが多くのアフリカの子どもたちの命を奪うだろう。
7. I **will** stay in Paris next week. 来週はパリに滞在しようと思う。
   (参考) **I'm going to stay** in Paris next week.
   I'm staying in Paris next week. 来週はパリに滞在する予定だ。
8. She **won't** speak about it. 彼女はそれについて話そうとしない。

▶ will は単純未来のほか、話し手の意志を含む未来「〜しようと思う」を表すことがあります。be going to や進行形で表す未来「〜する予定だ」は、それに向けてすでに準備していることを暗に示します。

▶ won't は拒絶を表します。

❷ 義務・推量・提案を表す助動詞　🎧 DL 39　💿 CD39

9. Every human being **must** eat to live. 人はみな生きるために食べなくてはならない。
10. There **must** be something wrong with the motor. モーターに不具合があるに違いない。

▶ must は9の意味のほか、10のように「〜に違いない」という強い推量の意味もあります。

11. You **should** protect yourself from mosquitoes. 蚊から身を守るようにすべきだ。
12. There **should** be no problem. まったく問題はないはずだ。

▶ 義務を表す助動詞には should, had better, ought to などがあります。should は、12のように「〜はずだ」という推量の意味もあります。

13. You **should** try the new Italian restaurant on the corner. 角の新しいイタリアンレストランに行ってみたらいいですよ。

▶ should は提案の意味でも用いられます。

Step 1 *Grammar Practice*

以下の英文について、(　　　) 内から適切な助動詞を選びましょう。

1. If you think you are wrong, you (will / should / might) apologize.
2. You (may / will / would) take a break at any time you want.
3. I made a big mistake yesterday. I (may / would / should) have acted on my boss's advice.
4. I (must / will / can) turn 50 next month, so I (can / must / may) care more about my health.
5. I've asked him to help us, but he (shouldn't / mustn't / won't).

 Step 2 *Create Sentences*

日本語の意味に合うように、(　　　) 内の語句を並べ替えましょう。

1. あなたは11時までに戻ってきて、お客様を待たなければなりません。
   (must / the guest / 11 o'clock / get / wait / by / for / you / back / and).

   _____

2. 次の京都行きの電車は5番線に到着します。
   (Platform 5 / be / next / at / Kyoto / arriving / to / will / the / train).

   _____

3. ブダペスト滞在中に温泉に行くといいですよ。
   (a hot spring area / should / stay / you / your / visit / during) in Budapest.

   _____

4. ティムの髪が濡れているので、外は雨が降っているに違いない。
   (Tim's / outside / so / raining / it / hair / be / is / wet / must / ,).

   _____

5. 昔はピアノを弾いていましたが、もう10年以上触っていません。
   (play / touched / used / 10 years / one / to / more / I / the piano / than / for / but / I / haven't / ,).

   _____

Step 3　Try Writing

日本語の意味に合わせて、[　　]内の語句を使って英文にしましょう。[　　]内の語句は形が変わる場合があります。

1. お名前を伺ってもよろしいでしょうか。[have]
   _____

2. そこに行くのはそんなに難しくないはずです。[get there]
   _____

3. 欲しい写真をどれでも持っていってもらって構いませんよ。[take]
   _____

4. 卒業したら、仕事を見つけなければなりません。[leave school]
   _____

5. もしあなたがこのことについてよく知っているのなら、説明会に来る必要はありません。[familiar with, orientation meeting]
   _____

Step 4　Write about Yourself

本文の 14 ～ 15 行目 "they should use the bed nets to protect themselves from mosquito bites" のように、「～すべきだ」、「～したほうがよい」という提案とその理由について、本文と以下の例を参考に、英語で短い文章を書いてみましょう。（助動詞 should を使いましょう。）

> 例1　You should go to the public library to concentrate on your homework. You won't get distracted in the quiet atmosphere there.
>
> 例2　You should go to bed earlier. I don't want to see you yawning many times during class.

Unit 11 May We Have a Catalog, Please?

▶ 仮定法

Model Essay 太字の表現に注意して読みましょう。 DL 40 CD 40

When purchasing a new house or car, we look through catalogs and choose from particular designs, colors, sizes and additional features. But consider this scenario: in the future, **if** you **were** able to choose your child's features from a catalog, **would** you? Or **would** you **leave** the result to mother nature?

Naturally, couples want their children to be healthy and relatively good-looking. It is also desirable that their offspring be intelligent in our increasingly competitive world. To realize these wishes, scientists are developing techniques that allow parents to select the genes of their babies — so-called "designer babies." **If** a couple **were to select** a combination of particular features, they **could have** a child that is close to their idea of perfection. After all, **if** the child **were** taller or smarter than average, **wouldn't** the parents **be** happier?

However, **if** gene selection **became** a reality, the high cost **would** probably **exclude** poorer couples from benefitting. Only the wealthy **would be** able to look through the "catalog of life" and select advantageous traits for their children. Naturally, this **would expand** the gap between the rich and poor even further. Moreover, can you imagine the scenario at a future Olympics whereby genetically designed people compete against those who are not? **If** you **had to guess** the winner of each event, it **would not be** too difficult, **would** it?

Notes

additional 追加の　　feature 特徴　　relatively 比較的、相対的に　　desirable 望ましい　　offspring 子孫　　increasingly ますます　　competitive 競い合う、競争の　　gene 遺伝子　　combination 組み合わせ　　reality 現実　　exclude 排除する、取り除く　　benefit 利益を得る　　wealthy 裕福な　　advantageous 有利な、好都合な　　trait 特性、資質　　compete 競う、競争する

Grammar for Writing! 仮定法

❶ 仮定を表す表現　　🎧 DL 41　💿 CD41

実際に起こりうることを仮定する場合には直説法を、起こりえないことを仮定する場合には仮定法を用います。仮定法では文の流れを変えるために if 節内の動詞を発話時の時制よりも一つ前の時制にすることがポイントです。

1. If it **rains** tomorrow, I **will stay** home and **relax**. 明日雨が降れば、家でゆっくりするだろう。
2. If I **were** in your shoes, I **would do** it right now.
   もし私が君の立場なら、すぐそれをするだろう。
3. If I **declined** the offer, I **could never get** such a big chance again.
   もしその申し出を断ったら、今後、そのような大きなチャンスを得ることはきっとないだろう。
4. If I **had practiced** more, I **could have given** a much better presentation.
   もしもっと練習していたら、私はよりよいプレゼンテーションができただろう。
5. If you **had declined** the offer, you **would be** still looking for a job.
   もしその申し出を断っていたら、あなたはいまだに仕事を探しているだろう。

- ▶ 直説法：「雨が降る」のように現実にありうる仮定の場合は、if 節内の動詞を現在形にし、主節の述部は単純未来の形を用います（1）。
- ▶ 仮定法過去：2 3 のように、現在の事実に反すること、今後起こりそうもないことについて仮定する場合に使います。
- ▶ 仮定法過去完了：4 のように、過去の事実に反することについて、仮定する場合に使います。
- ▶ 過去の事実に対して現在についての仮定をする（「過去に〜していたら今…なのに」）場合は、5 の形になります。

❷ 仮定法を用いた表現　　🎧 DL 42　💿 CD42

仮定法を用いた慣用的な表現があります。if 節を用いないものもあります。

6. I **wish** I **had** enough time to consider this. この件を検討する時間が十分あればよいのですが。
7. If a couple **were to select** a combination of particular features, they could have a "perfect" baby. 仮に夫婦が特定の性質を選ぶことができるなら、いわゆる『完璧な』子どもを持つことができるだろう。
8. I think it **would be** nice to have lunch here. ここで昼食を食べたら素敵かと思いますが。

- ▶ 〈wish ＋仮定法〉は「〜ならよいのに」という願望を表します。
- ▶ if 節で用いられる were to は、より「現実離れした仮定の話」であることを示します（7）。
- ▶ 助動詞 would は発言を和らげる働きもあり、絶対的な提案でないことを示せます（8）。

9. **Without** your support, we **would fail**. あなたの支援がなければ、私たちは失敗するだろう。
10. **A wise couple wouldn't** think about such a thing.
    賢い夫婦ならそんなことを考えないだろう。

- ▶ if 節がなくても、without を使ったり（9）、主語の中に仮定の意味を含めることで（10）、仮定の意味を表します。

Unit 11　May We Have a Catalog, Please?

Step 1　Grammar Practice

[　]内の語を正しい形にして、（　）内に書き入れましょう。

1. If it (　　　　　) not for this dictionary, I wouldn't be able to understand the story in this book.　[be]
2. Without your suggestion, I (　　　　　) for this position last year.　[won't apply]
3. If it (　　　　　) freezing outside, I don't want to walk to the office.　[be]
4. Should Stacey leave office, I (　　　　　) on the project instead of her.　[will work]
5. If I (　　　　　) harder, I could have passed the test.　[study]

Step 2　Create Sentences

日本語の意味に合わせて、（　）内の語句を並べ替えましょう。

1. たとえあなたが英語が得意でも、彼女の小説は読みにくいと思うよ。
   (hard / good at / even / think / her novel / are / if / I / you / is / to read / English / ,).

2. 私はもしアドバイスを求められたら、彼女がそれをするべきだと言うつもりです。
   (asked / should / I / do / if / would / for / advice / were / she / I / say / it / ,).

3. 万が一私たちが会議の日を変更したら、彼らは怒るだろう。
   (they / annoyed / if / the date / we / to / change / were / be / the meeting / of / would / ,).

4. その件について彼らと話をしていたら、あのような大きな間違いはしなかっただろう。
   (the matter / discussed / made / had / if / a / we / big mistake / with them / such / wouldn't / we / have / ,).

5. この種の仕事には、バーバラが最適任者ではないかと思います。
   (would / work / I / Barbara / best / kind / think / of / person / the / be / this / for).

Step 3 Try Writing

日本語の意味に合わせて、[ ]内の語句を使って英文にしましょう。[ ]内の語句は形が変わる場合があります。

1. もし彼が中国語を話せるのなら、私たちは彼を雇うのだが。[hire]
   _____

2. コンピュータがなければ、この世はどうなるだろう。[the world]
   _____

3. もしあなたの手紙が昨日届いていたら、今日彼に渡せるのに。[pass]
   _____

4. 早急にお返事いただけると幸いです。[appreciate, reply]
   _____

5. 韓国語で自分の言いたいことを伝えられるといいのですが。[make]
   _____

Step 4 Write about Yourself

本文の 9 〜 10 行目 "If a couple were to select a combination of particular features, they could have a child that is close to their idea of perfection." のように、あなたの願望について、本文と以下の例を参考に、英語で短い文章を書いてみましょう。

> 例1　If I could receive a scholarship, I would like to go to Australia and study English there. I believe that the clean air and the beauty of nature would boost my motivation to study.
>
> 例2　If I were to go back to a time in the past, I would go back to the Meiji period. I would like to see the *Bunmei-kaika*, or cultural enlightenment, with my own eyes.

Unit 11 May We Have a Catalog, Please?

Unit 12 Bright Little Lights

➡ 接続詞

Model Essay 太字の表現に注意して読みましょう。

Despite their vital role in nature, insects seem to have relatively few friends among humans. For instance, **when** a fly, bee **or** spider appears, we often try to avoid, remove **or** destroy it immediately. **But** in some parts of the world, one kind of insect is being widely praised **and** carefully protected for the prosperity it brings.

In the past, the small town of Nanacamilpa in Mexico saw only a handful of tourists **because** there was little to do **or** see there. Nowadays the picture is very different. Thanks to fireflies, it has been transformed from a ghost town to the most visited town in its state, with around 100,000 visitors every year.

On summer nights, fireflies that inhabit the nearby forests of Tlaxcala provide a magical display of light. This is what attracts the tourists **and** their much-needed currency. To see the display, the visitors must walk quietly along forest trails in complete darkness, **so** no phones **or** flashlights are allowed. At times, the trails can be steep **and** muddy, **and** the rain can be cold. Even so, the tourists keep coming.

Firefly tourism is also growing in Japan, Taiwan, Malaysia **and** parts of the eastern US. **Although** very small, the bright insects are demonstrating **that** the wonder of nature is a powerful magnet for human curiosity.

Notes

vital 極めて重要な　praise 賞賛する　prosperity 繁栄　Nanacamilpa ナナカミルパ（メキシコのトラスカラ州にある町）　a handful of わずかな　firefly ホタル　transform 変化させる　inhabit 生息する　Tlaxcala トラスカラ（メキシコにある州）　much-needed 切望していた　currency 貨幣　trail 小道、登山道　at times 時々　steep 急勾配の　muddy ぬかるんだ　demonstrate 証明する　magnet 引きつけるもの

Grammar for Writing! 接続詞

❶ 等位接続詞
🎧 DL 44　💿 CD44

等位接続詞は語や句、節どうしを対等な関係で結ぶ働きをします。

① One kind of insect is being widely praised **and** carefully protected.
　　　　　　　　　　　　　ある種類の昆虫が広く賞賛され、注意深く保護されている。

② This machine is easy to handle, **so** you can use it.
　　　　　　　　　　　　　　　この機械は扱いやすいので、あなたも使えますよ。

▶ ①では接続詞 and が widely praised と carefully protected を対等に結んでいます。
▶ ②は因果関係を示します。so は〈原因, so 結果〉の形で使います。

③ We often try to avoid, remove **or** destroy it immediately.
　　　　　　　　　　　私たちはよくそれを避けたり、排除したり、あるいはすぐに殺したりする。

④ It's neither warm **nor** cold. 暖かくもなければ寒くもない。

▶ ③では接続詞 or が to 不定詞の後の3つの動詞を結んでいます。
▶ neither A nor B で「A も B もない」という意味を表します（④）。either A or B「A か B のいずれか」という表現もあります。

⑤ It's an old car, **but** it hardly ever breaks down. 古い車ですが、めったに壊れない。

⑥ She tried hard, **yet** she couldn't find any evidence.
　　　　　　　　　　　　　　彼女は一生懸命取り組んだが、何も証拠は得られなかった。

⑦ The sales of his company have dropped; **however**, he never thinks of getting out of the business. 彼の会社の売り上げが落ち込んでいるが、彼は廃業することをまったく考えていない。

▶ 逆接を表す接続詞には but や yet があります。副詞の however でも同様の意味を表せますが、however は副詞で、主に書き言葉で用いられ、逆接の意味をより際立たせます。

❷ 従位接続詞
🎧 DL 45　💿 CD45

従位接続詞は、主節に従属する名詞節または副詞節を導きます。

⑧ We believe **that** this project will go well. この企画はうまくいくと信じている。

⑨ I'm wondering **whether/if** I should go there. そこに行くべきかどうか迷っている。

▶ that は「～すること」という名詞節を、whether/if は「～するかどうか」という名詞節を導きます。

⑩ **When** a fly or bee appears, we often try to avoid it.
　　　　　　　　　　　　　　ハエやハチが現れたら、しばしば避けようとする。

⑪ That town saw only a handful of tourists **because** there was little to do there.
　　　　　　　　　　　その町にはすることがほとんどなかったので、一握りの旅行者しか見られなかった。

⑫ **Although** they are small, they are strong. それらはとても小さいが、強い。

▶ ⑩～⑫は副詞節を導く従位接続詞です。代表的なものに、時（when, as, while など）、理由（because, since など）、譲歩（although, though など）、条件（if, unless など）を表すものがあります。

Step 1　Grammar Practice

以下の英文の（　）に入る適切な語を、選択肢から選びましょう。選択肢には、使われない語句も含まれています。

1. I'd like to visit your office (　　　　　) that's all right with you.
2. Turn right at that corner (　　　　　) you will find the store on your left.
3. He stayed up late last night, (　　　　　) he couldn't get up early this morning.
4. You can never lose weight (　　　　　) you do regular exercise.
5. I think either Ken (　　　　　) Lucy is in charge of this matter.

if	unless	while	but
and	or	so	because

 Step 2　Create Sentences

日本語の意味に合うように、（　）内の語句を並べ替えましょう。

1. いったん何かに取り組み始めたら、最後まで終えるべきです。
   (you / working / finish / once / on / you / it / something / start / should / ,).

   _____

2. 私は疲れ果てていましたが、宿題をしなければなりませんでした。
   (homework / exhausted / yet / I / had / was / I / do / to / my / ,).

   _____

3. 明日までに私の報告書を見ていただけないかと思っているのですが。
   (if / my report / I / check / wondering / by / could / you / was / tomorrow).

   _____

4. 私の母は気分が悪かったので、何も食べませんでした。
   (because / my mother / sick / nothing / she / ate / feeling / was).

   _____

5. 電車が通っていないので、そこに行くにはタクシーを使わなければなりません。
   (there / no / a taxi / so / are / have to / you'll / there / trains / to / take / get / ,).

   _____

Step 3 Try Writing

日本語の意味に合わせて、[   ]内の語句を使って英文にしましょう。[   ]内の語句は形が変わる場合があります。

1. 彼のお父さんもお母さんも日本語を話しません。[neither]

   _____

2. いくつかのデータによると、歩くことが健康によいということです。[suggest]

   _____

3. これがその問題に対する1つの解決策ですが、他にもあるはずです。[however]

   _____

4. 渋滞がひどかったので、我々はミーティングに遅れてしまいました。[heavy traffic]

   _____

5. お互い長い間会っていませんが、今でもとてもよい友だちどうしです。[for ages]

   _____

Step 4 Write about Yourself

本文の6～7行目 "In the past, the small town of Nanacamilpa in Mexico saw only a handful of tourists because there was little to do or see there." のように、過去と現在で変化したこととその理由について、本文と以下の例を参考に、英語で短い文章を書いてみましょう。

> 例1 In the past, the university cafeteria was always crowded with students because that was the only place where we could eat lunch. However, it is not the only place now, since a shopping mall was opened in this neighborhood.
>
> 例2 In the past, we saw pillar posts everywhere in Japan. However, we rarely see them now because they are out of production.

Unit 12 Bright Little Lights

Unit 13 Popular but Penniless

■▶ 不定詞と動名詞

Model Essay 太字の表現に注意して読みましょう。 🎧 DL 46 💿 CD 46

Many young people today aspire **to become** rich and famous in the music entertainment field. For the minority who are successful, there are two celebrities **to remind** them of a certain pitfall.

The singer and dancer Michael Jackson was arguably one of the most
5 successful entertainers of all time. However, he enjoyed **spending** money on extravagant and bizarre items. Consequently, in the years just before his death in 2009, the performing genius was almost bankrupt and had many debts **to repay**. For such a global superstar, bankruptcy would have been
10 a shameful end to a brilliant career. Therefore, in order **to avoid** this fate, Jackson borrowed millions of dollars from wealthy friends. In the end, however, it is said he died with debts of around 450 million dollars.

15 **Being** famous and broke is not only a phenomenon of modern times. Mozart, possibly the most famous composer ever, died penniless in 1791 and was buried in a very simple and ordinary grave. The musical genius always worked hard **to earn** money, and his collective earnings actually put him
20 among the top five wealthiest people of his time. Yet, Mozart's extravagant tastes in later life also left him with no money.

Therefore, regardless of your career path in life, if you become wealthy, try **to remember** the carelessness of these two giants and look after your hard-earned money wisely.

Notes

penniless 一文無しの　aspire 熱望する　celebrity 有名人　pitfall わな　extravagant 派手な
bizarre 奇怪な　consequently その結果　genius 天才　bankrupt 破産した　debt 借金　repay 返済する　shameful 恥ずべき　fate 運命　broke 破産して、一文無しで　phenomenon 現象
bury 埋葬する　grave 墓　extravagant taste 浪費癖　regardless of ～にもかかわらず

Grammar for Writing! 不定詞と動名詞

❶ to 不定詞

不定詞は文中で名詞、形容詞または副詞の働きをします。

1. Many people want **to become** rich and famous. 多くの人は裕福で有名になりたい。
2. He had many debts **to repay**. 彼には返済すべき借金がたくさんあった。
3. The musician worked hard **to earn** money. その音楽家はお金を稼ぐために一生懸命働いた。
4. My grandmother lived **to be** 100 years old. 私の祖母は100歳まで生きた。
5. It's very kind of you **to say** that. そんなことを言ってくれるなんて、君は優しいね。
6. I'm very surprised **to hear** the news. 私はその知らせを聞いて、とても驚いている。

▶ to 不定詞には①の名詞的用法（〜すること）、②の形容詞的用法（〜するための、〜するべき）、③の副詞的用法（〜するために）の3つの基本用法があります。
▶ 副詞的用法の中には、「〜したその結果…だった」という結果の意味や（④）、判断・根拠の基準や感情の原因を示すものがあります（⑤⑥）。

❷ 動名詞

動名詞は文中で名詞の働きをします。

7. **Being** famous and broke is not only a phenomenon of modern times. 有名かつ一文無しであることは現代に限った現象ではない。
8. He enjoyed **spending** a lot of money. 彼は多くのお金を使うことを楽しんだ。

❸ 動詞の目的語になる不定詞と動名詞

動詞によって目的語に to 不定詞を取るか、動名詞を取るかが決まります。

9. He refused **to answer** the question. 彼は質問に答えることを拒んだ。
10. I finished **writing** the report. 私はレポートを書き終えた。
11. Did you remember **to pick up** the tickets? チケットを忘れずに受け取ってきましたか。
12. I remember **turning off** my alarm clock this morning. 今朝、目覚まし時計を止めたことを覚えている。
13. She likes **to take** [**taking**] photos. 彼女は写真を撮るのが好きだ。

▶ to 不定詞のみ取る動詞（⑨）：aim, decide, expect, hope, promise, refuse, want など
▶ 動名詞のみ取る動詞（⑩）：avoid, deny, finish, mind, quit, give up, put off など
▶ ⑪⑫の remember のように to 不定詞と動名詞で意味が変わる動詞もあります。to 不定詞の「（これから）〜することを覚えている」対し、動名詞は「〜したことを覚えている」となります。
▶ ⑬の like のように to 不定詞でも動名詞でもあまり意味が変わらない動詞もあります。

Step 1 Grammar Practice

以下の英文の [　] 内の語を正しい形にして、(　) 内に書き入れましょう。

1. Can you give her something cold (　　　　　　　　)? She looks thirsty. [drink]
2. Mike denies (　　　　　　　　) the window, but I believe he did it. [break]
3. The heavy rain prevented us from (　　　　　　　　) on a picnic. [go]
4. Please don't hesitate (　　　　　　　　) me if you have any questions. [ask]
5. I remember (　　　　　　　　) a lot on my first day of elementary school as if it were just yesterday. [cry]

Step 2 Create Sentences

日本語の意味に合わせて、(　) 内の語句を並べ替えましょう。

1. 残念ながら、今月末に退職することをあなたにお伝えします。
(say / end / that / I / regret / at / leave / the / I / to / company / will / the) of this month.

2. 今お時間があるようでしたら、あなたにお話したいことがあるのですが。
(something / available / I / you / if / tell / now / are / to / have / you).

3. スーは来月に行われる自分の結婚式の準備で忙しい。
(preparing / wedding / her / is / Sue / next month / for / busy).

4. お店がいつも混んでいるので、土曜日には買い物に行かないようにしています。
(avoid / on Saturdays / the shops / going / busy / I / try / are / because / to / shopping / always).

5. あなたが4月に日本に戻ってくると聞いて嬉しく思っています。
(glad / in April / you'll / that / to Japan / I'm / hear / coming / be / to / back).

Step 3 Try Writing

日本語の意味に合わせて、[　]内の語句を使って英文にしましょう。[　]内の語句は形が変わる場合があります。

1. 交通渋滞を避けるために、早めに出発しましょう。[traffic]

   _____

2. 家に帰る途中で牛乳を買ってくることを忘れないでね。[forget]

   _____

3. 海外で数年働きたいですか。[would, work overseas]

   _____

4. 人前でスピーチをすることには慣れていません。[used]

   _____

5. よろしければ、今夜夕食を作るのを手伝いますよ。[help]

   _____

Step 4 Write about Yourself

本文の18〜19行目 "The musical genius always worked hard to earn money" のように、あなたが一生懸命取り組んだこととその目的について、本文と以下の例を参考に、英語で短い文章を書いてみましょう。

 例1　I worked hard to remove waste from the river with my friends. Now that it has clean water, I hope the fish will come back.

例2　I practiced day after day to produce my best performance at the piano contest. Then, on the day of the contest, I didn't make any mistakes.

Unit 14 Taxing the Robots

▶ 受動態

Model Essay 太字の表現に注意して読みましょう。

In industrialized countries, it **is** often **said** that employees do not have enough personal leisure time. Yet, with advances in robotic technology, this desire may become a reality sooner than we think. If so, is it one that workers will actually enjoy and governments will welcome?

Since the 1970s, the use of robotic technology has cut human labor requirements in various business sectors, especially the car industry. In factories, while heavy and repetitive tasks **are done** by robots, those involving logical thinking and decision-making **are** primarily **done** by humans. But with the rapid development of Artificial Intelligence (AI), robots that are able to think and act like humans will occupy many more positions across various industries. In fact, it has **been estimated** that about one-third of all jobs currently done by humans could disappear by 2030. If this happens, will the unemployed people really enjoy their abundant free time, or will they get bored?

And what about governments? One consequence of job losses to AI robots concerns income tax. Taxes **are paid** by workers, but when robots replace humans, governments will not receive that vital income to provide facilities and services for their citizens. Therefore, some people have proposed that robot staff pay income tax, the same as human workers. Otherwise, how can society function in the future?

Notes

industrialize 産業化する　robotic technology ロボット工学　sector 分野、業種　Artificial Intelligence (AI) 人工知能　estimate 見積もる　currently 現在、目下　unemployed 失業中の　abundant 豊富な　get bored 退屈する　consequence 結果、帰結　job loss 失業　concern 〜に関係する　income tax 所得税　function 機能する

Grammar for Writing! 受動態

❶ 受動態を使う場合　　DL 51　CD51

受動態は「ある動作・行為をされる側」に注目し、「Sは〜される」と述べるときに使います。「動作・行為をする側」を示さなくても文にすることができます。

1. Repetitive tasks **are done** by robots. 繰り返しの作業はロボットによって行われている。
2. English and French **are spoken** in Canada. カナダでは英語とフランス語が使われている。
3. The grocery store **was robbed** last night. 昨晩、その食料雑貨店には泥棒が入った。
4. In the study, 30 male students **were selected** as participants.
その研究では30人の男子学生が参加者として選ばれた。

▶ ある行為について「される側」に注目したいとき、受動態を使います。by で動作主を表すこともありますが（1）、動作主が不明または言うまでもないときは示す必要はありません（2 3）。
▶ 「する側」を示す必要がない受動態は、何かを客観的に述べるのに向いています。研究を扱った論文（4）や新聞記事、公共の場での掲示文など、客観性が求められる文では受動態が役立ちます。

5. One consequence of job losses to AI robots concerns income tax. Taxes **are paid by workers**. (△ Workers pay taxes.)   AIロボットに負けて仕事を失う影響の1つは所得税に関係する。税金は労働者によって支払われているのだ。

▶ 2つ目の文は能動態でも表せますが、受動態が好まれます。前の文で tax について述べているので、次の文では taxes を主語に置くことで、2つの文のつながりが明確になります。

❷ 受動態でよくある間違い　　DL 52　CD52

6. Jamal **was laughed at** [× was laughed] by all the people there.
ジャマールはそこにいた人々全員から笑われた。
7. The parcel **arrived** [× was arrived] a couple of hours ago.
その小包は2時間ほど前に届いた。

▶ 句動詞を受動態にする場合、前置詞や副詞などを省略しないように気をつけます（6）。
▶ 受動態にできるのは他動詞です。自動詞は受動態にできないので注意しましょう（7）。

❸ 受動態を使った様々な表現　　DL 53　CD53

8. Her achievements **are known to** many people. 彼女の業績は多くの人々に知られている。
9. **It is** often **said that** employees do not have enough personal leisure time.
会社に勤務する人は、個人的な余暇を十分にとることはできないとよく言われている。

▶ be known to のように by 以外の前置詞を用いる表現もあります（8）。
▶ It is ＋過去分詞＋ that 節：過去分詞には said「言われている」（9）、estimated「見積もられている」、believed「考えられている」、expected「予想されている」などがきます。

Unit 14　Taxing the Robots

Step 1　Grammar Practice

以下の英文の（　）には動詞が入ります。文中の要素を手掛かりにして、適切な述語を選択肢から選び、適切な形に変えて書き入れましょう。

1. It (　　　　　　　　) that hot springs are great for recovering from fatigue and improving overall health.
2. Mr. Chang is one of our important clients. His name (　　　　　　　　) to everybody in this firm.
3. The pretty cat (　　　　　　　　) by the owner of the barber shop.
4. This book (　　　　　　　　) in easy English, so I think you can read it.
5. If headaches (　　　　　　　　) so often, you should see your doctor.

write　　occur　　say　　know　　take care of

 Step 2　Create Sentences

日本語の意味に合わせて、（　）内の語句を並べ替えましょう。

1. 彼の絵は来週、市の美術館に展示されます。
   (drawing / next week / city museum / in / his / displayed / the / be / will).

   _____

2. 彼女は同僚に、通りを渡っているところを見られました。
   (crossing / her colleagues / by / she / the street / seen / was).

   _____

3. 高校生がこのロボットを作ったということに私はとても驚いています。
   (high school / made / very surprised / was / I'm / students / that / this / robot / by).

   _____

4. ネイザンは凍った道で転んでけがをしました。
   (Nathan / hurt / icy / the / slipped / road / and / got / on).

   _____

5. 私は若いときは兄に似ていましたが、今は似ていません。
   (look / resembled / young / I was / I / now / different / but / when / we / my brother / ,).

   _____

Step 3　Try Writing

日本語の意味に合わせて、[　　]内の語句を使って英文にしましょう。[　　]内の語句は形が変わる場合があります。

1. 次の会議は金曜日の夕方に開かれます。[hold]

   _____

2. この建物内は禁煙です。[allow]

   _____

3. 関東の人はそばが好きですが、関西の人はうどんを好んで食べると言われています。
   [Kansai people, say]

   _____

4. その交通事故で負傷した人は誰もいませんでした。[injure]

   _____

5. 電車は間もなくここに到着するでしょう。[arrive]

   _____

Step 4　Write about Yourself

本文の1〜2行目 "it is often said that employees do not have enough personal leisure time" のように、世の中でよく言われていることとそれに対する自分の意見について、本文と以下の例を参考に、英語で短い文章を書いてみましょう。

> 例1　It is said that more and more people use e-mail rather than write letters. However, I believe that a handwritten letter can convey a warm message like "you are special to me."
>
> 例2　It is said that international tourists to Japan have increased by 30%. I'd like to improve my language skills and talk with them in their native languages.

Unit 14　Taxing the Robots

Unit 15 Sayonara, My Dear

▶ 強調・倒置・形式主語

Model Essay　太字の表現に注意して読みましょう。　DL 54　CD 54

"Sayonara, my dear, sayonara." These were reportedly the last words spoken by Ranald MacDonald when he died in the US in 1894, aged 70. However, **it is** strange **that** he used Japanese, since he was obviously not from Japan.

During his childhood, MacDonald's relatives often told him fascinating stories about Japan, saying their ancestors might have come from Asia. He must have found **it** exciting **to** listen to the stories, and dreamt of traveling there. No doubt **it was** this strong desire **that** brought him to the country in July 1848, at the age of around 23.

However, **never did he imagine** that his welcome would be hostile. He was caught by samurai and, as a prisoner, **off he was sent to Nagasaki**, the only place where trading with Dutch ships was allowed. American and British ships were eager to trade with Japan, too, but the obstacle was that no Japanese spoke English. Yet, **it was** MacDonald's Japanese ability **that** resolved the communication problem. He had been studying the language in prison and was asked to teach English to fourteen Japanese men.

Within a year, MacDonald was released and he returned to America. Writing to Congress, he praised Japanese society and its kind people. As a result of his English lessons and his praise, communication and trade with Japan flourished. Thus, his efforts should not be forgotten in books on the history of Japan.

Notes

reportedly 伝えられたところ　Ranald MacDonald ラナルド・マクドナルド（冒険家。日本が鎖国の時代にアメリカの捕鯨船からボートで日本に密入国した）　obviously 明らかに　childhood 子ども時代、幼少期　relative 親戚　fascinating 魅力的な　ancestor 先祖　desire 希望、要望　hostile 敵意を持った　prisoner 囚人　obstacle 障害　resolve 解決する　release 釈放する　Congress （アメリカの）国会　flourish 繁盛する、栄える

Grammar for Writing! 強調・倒置・形式主語

❶ 強調に伴う倒置

否定語や強調したい語句を文頭に置くことがあります。その場合、あとに続く主語と動詞の順番が逆になり、疑問文の語順になります（倒置）。

1. Never **did he imagine** that his welcome would be hostile.
   彼の歓迎が敵意を持ったものになるとは、まったく想像していなかった。
2. Never again **will I vote** for him. 私は二度と彼には投票しない。
3. Only then **did I realize** that I had made a mistake.
   そのときになって初めて、私は間違いを犯していたとわかった。
4. Behind the forest **stands a little lodge**. 森の後ろに小さなロッジがある。

   ▶ 否定語が文頭に出た倒置：〈否定語＋ be 動詞/助動詞 ＋主語＋動詞〉の形になります（1 2）。
   ▶ 時や場所を表す副詞句も、強調のために文頭に置かれることがあります（3 4）。

❷ 強調構文

ある語句や節を強調したい場合、it is ～ that ... の～の位置に強調したい語句や節を置いて表すことができます（強調構文）。

5. **It was** MacDonald's Japanese ability **that** resolved the communication problem.
   コミュニケーションの問題を解決したのは、マクドナルドの日本語力だった。
6. **It is** after lunch **that** I will meet my client. 顧客に会うのは昼食後だ。

   ▶ it is ～ that ... の～の位置に名詞句や前置詞句、副詞句などを置いて強調することができます。強調される語句が that 節から離れて～の位置に来ることから、「分裂文」と呼ばれることもあります。

❸ 形式主語・形式目的語

形式主語 it には意味がなく、本来この位置に来るべき語句が後ろにあることを示します。

7. **It** is strange that he used Japanese. 彼が日本語を使ったのは奇妙である。
8. **It** is important to stay positive in order to write a good essay.
   よいエッセイを書くには、前向きな気持ちでいることが重要である。

   ▶ 7 や 8 の that 節や不定詞句を主語の位置に置くと、重たくなるため、仮の主語 it が用いられています。

9. She must have found **it** exciting to listen to the stories.
   彼女はそのいろんな話を聞くことはおもしろいと思ったに違いない。
10. I took **it** for granted that our bonuses would increase.
    当然、ボーナスは増えると思っていましたよ。

    ▶ it は形式目的語としても用いられ、それぞれ後の不定詞句や that 節を指します。

Unit 15 Sayonara, My Dear

Step 1 *Grammar Practice*

以下の英文を [　] の指示に従って書き換えましょう。

1. I have never felt so alone. [never を文頭に置く]

___

2. My wife always gives me good advice. [it を用いて my wife を強調する文に]

___

3. To keep working on the project is important. [形式主語 it を用いる]

___

4. It is difficult to finish this work. [I find から始まる文に]

___

5. You could buy it at half price. [only yesterday を加えて、it を用いた強調構文に]

___

 Step 2 *Create Sentences*

日本語の意味に合わせて、(　) 内の語句を並べ替えましょう。

1. あなたがここに来るなんて、夢にも思いませんでした。
(I / dream / here / that / would / did / come / you / little).

___

2. ハロルドが私たちに薦めていたのはこのレストランです。
(restaurant / is / that / Harold / it / to / this / recommended / us).

___

3. 昨日まで、私たちはそのコンピュータの問題には気付いていませんでした。
Not (until / the computer / did / we / problem / yesterday / notice).

___

4. このパーティーではネクタイを着用する必要はありません。
(necessary / this / wear / not / a tie / party / it / to / is / at).

___

5. 1日中コンピュータの仕事をするのは退屈です。
(it / computer work / all / do / find / I / boring / day / to).

___

Step 3　Try Writing

日本語の意味に合わせて、[　]内の語句を使って英文にしましょう。[　]内の語句は形が変わる場合があります。

1. このファイルを私たちのウェブサイトからダウンロードするのは簡単です。[it]

2. 私は彼女とうまくやっていくのは難しいと感じています。[find, along]

3. 夏休みに訪れたいのはニューヨークです。[it]

4. テストで満点を取るなんて、まったく夢にも思いませんでした。[never, did]

5. 私は毎朝早く起きるようにしています [make, rule]

Step 4　Write about Yourself

本文の10行目の "never did he imagine that his welcome would be hostile" のように、思いかけず起こったことやできるようになったことについて、本文と以下の例を参考に、英語で短い文章を書いてみましょう。

> 例1　Never did I think that I could swim the crawl for 50 meters. Now I want to try the backstroke.
>
> 例2　Never did I expect that some sumo wrestlers would stay near my house during the tournament next week. I'm looking forward to seeing them up close.

Unit 15　Sayonara, My Dear

本書には CD（別売）があります

Writing Key
English Grammar and Usage for Better Writing
英語の感覚をつかむ 文法からライティングへ

2019年1月20日 初版第1刷発行
2024年3月30日 初版第8刷発行

著 者 　北尾　泰幸
　　　　Anthony Allan

発行者 　福岡　正人
発行所 　株式会社 金星堂
（〒101-0051）東京都千代田区神田神保町 3-21
Tel.（03）3263-3828（営業部）
　　（03）3263-3997（編集部）
Fax（03）3263-0716
https://www.kinsei-do.co.jp

編集担当／蔦原美智　　　　　　　Printed in Japan
印刷所／日新印刷株式会社　製本所／松島製本
本書の無断複製・複写は著作権法上での例外を除き禁じられています。本書を代行業者等の第三者に依頼してスキャンやデジタル化することは、たとえ個人や家庭内での利用であっても認められておりません。
落丁・乱丁本はお取り替えいたします。

ISBN978-4-7647-4086-0　C1082